Contents

The New Alchemists

The New Alchemists

Charles Handy

Photographed by Elizabeth Handy

HUTCHINSON
London

First published in the United Kingdom in 1999
by Hutchinson

The Random House Group Limited
20 Vauxhall Bridge Road, London SW1V 2SA

Random House Australia (Pty) Limited
20 Alfred Street, Milsons Point, Sydney
New South Wales 2061, Australia

Random House New Zealand Limited
18 Poland Road, Glenfield,
Auckland 10, New Zealand

Random House South Africa (Pty) Limited
Endulini, 5A Jubilee Road, Parktown 2193,
South Africa

The Random House Group Limited Reg. No. 954009
www.randomhouse.co.uk

A CIP catalogue record for this book
is available from the British Library

Papers used by Random House are natural, recyclable products made from wood grown in sustainable forests. The manufacturing processes conform to the environmental regulations of the country of origin

ISBN 0 09 180215 6

Design/make-up by Roger Walker

Typeset in 11/16pt Poppl-Pontifex

Printed and bound in Great Britain by
Butler & Tanner Limited, Frome and London

To Kate and Scott
and a life of alchemy

Acknowledgements

We are hugely indebted to the twenty-nine individuals who agreed to be featured in this book. All busy people, they gave us generously of their time, shared large chunks of their private life stories with us and welcomed us into their homes or workplaces. Without their help and encouragement this book would never have been possible. The book is all about people, and we have been fortunate in meeting such a diverse and interesting selection.

A book like this is a complicated one to produce. Our publishers at Random House, headed by the inspirational Gail Rebuck, have made it seem easy as well as enjoyable. Paul Sidey, our editor, has masterminded the management of the whole project and has enriched the book with his insights, his care for its quality and his enthusiasm. The printers, Butler and Tanner, are crucial to a work of this sort and we are immensely grateful to them, and to Stephen Rose in particular, for their skill as well as for their interest in the photographs. Martin Thornton and Richard O'Dwyer, of Shades in London, made the original prints for the composite portraits, often working to tight deadlines to meet our requirements. We are very grateful to them both.

It is no use producing a book if no-one knows of its existence. Fiona Spencer Thomas, backed by the marketing staff of Random House, has been tireless in her efforts to spread the news of the book, while Rachel Ward and the people at the Association of MBAs have made it possible to show the book to audiences around the country. Ultimately, however, we depend on the individuals who work in book stores up and down the country to promote our work. Our thanks go, in advance, to our many friends in the book trade.

We hope that people will find the book as enjoyable and inspiring to read as we have found it to produce.

Charles and Elizabeth Handy
London and Norfolk, Summer 1999

Introduction

ALCHEMY

This book is a collection of twenty-nine interesting and original individuals, portrayed in both photographs and words. We call them the New Alchemists because they have each created something significant out of nothing or turned the equivalent of base metal into a kind of gold. They are metaphorical, not literal, alchemists. Unlike the alchemists of old, however, these New Alchemists are not frauds, nor is money usually their main motive. Those in our small group include several individuals who make whole businesses out of nothing, others who create visionary buildings where once there was only wasteland, found pioneering institutions, start drama festivals, develop new forms of health care and innovative charities. They transform schools, bring new airlines into being, invent life-saving devices, produce works of great art or new galleries of art.

There are many other successful people in society, people who have reached high levels in their organizations or found distinction in the course of their jobs. This book is not about them. It is about those who create something special out of their own imagination. Alchemy of this sort has always been a crucial part of progress. Think of the vacuum cleaner, invented by the British engineer Hubert Cecil Booth in 1902, and now greatly improved by James Dyson, or the World Wide Web, invented by another Britisher, Tim Berners-Lee, or institutions like the Samaritans, again the idea of one man, Chad Varah.

Today, more than ever, we need more such alchemists in society, at all levels and in all sectors. They sow the seeds of the future. Innovation and creativity, enterprise and entrepreneurship are the vogue words for the new millennium. Alchemy itself is becoming a popular metaphor; there is even a new venture capital business calling itself Alchemy. But these brave words need special individuals to deliver them. Rhetoric by itself is not enough. Who are these people and how do they become what they are? What sets them going? What keeps them going?

11

Less grandly, in a world where 'jobs' as we used to know them will be in short supply, more people need to think of creating their own work, as most of these people have done. By examining the stories of our chosen alchemists we can learn more about the problems facing more ordinary alchemists, those who open their own shops, start a business or become self-employed. How did our chosen alchemists go about it? What early experiences or people gave them the confidence to set out on their own? What trials and tribulations did they face? From where do they draw their strength? How could it have been made easier?

This is not a new subject. There are many essays and reports written on it, numerous analyses of business and even social entrepreneurs. Our aim is different. The purpose and the hope behind the book is that others may see this selection of alchemists as models or even heroes, whose examples they might follow in their own lives. For these were, and still are, ordinary people who have gone on to do extraordinary things. It is often easier to learn from example than from precept or theory if we can personally identify with the examples. The stories told here should give encouragement to anyone who has ever suffered from dyslexia, or failed exams, been turned down for a job or a loan, made bankrupt, been sacked or passed over for promotion. All these things have happened to one or other of the alchemists and turned out not to be the obstacles that they seemed at the time.

The twenty-nine individuals deliberately cover a wide range. The oldest is in his eighties, the youngest are in their early thirties. Some are household names, some are known only in their own spheres of work. Some have comfortable, even privileged, backgrounds but many have not. One comes from Italy, one from New Zealand, one is of Asian origin, two have parents who came from the Caribbean and one from Ghana. Eight are women, a smaller percentage than we expected, something which calls for comment later on in the book.

They are all Londoners. This is partly because we live in London and wanted to investigate the extent of alchemy around us. We were surprised by how much there was. We could have made the book five times bigger, so many were the examples quoted to us. This was not, however, intended to be in any way a complete register of every new alchemist in London but only a representative sample.

There was also another reason for confining the search to London, which we broadly defined as falling within the scope of the street maps of that city. We wondered whether the place and the time makes a difference. Is there something about, for instance, Athens in the fifth century BC or Florence in the fifteenth century, which might be true of London at the end of this millennium: a culture and an atmosphere which attract and encourage alchemy of all sorts?

We cannot prove anything without doing a major comparative study of other cities but we think it likely that alchemists may cluster where creativity of different kinds flourishes, where there is a local appetite for innovation and the products of innovation, where there are centres of finance and of political influence. Alchemy often requires supportive networks to be successful at first. London has all of these. If this be true, the implications for policy are considerable and will be addressed in a later chapter. The study, therefore, may have London as its focus but its messages, we believe, are universal. Forget the names, remember the stories.

We talked only to the individuals themselves, not to colleagues or competitors or other commentators. We were interested in what it was in their lives that influenced them to be alchemists rather than to pursue a more traditional career. This information could only come from them, from their recollections of their early lives, of the people and experiences that shaped them. They are all, obviously, successful in their own spheres but we do not know what it is like to work with them or for them, or even to live with them. We are dependent on their answers for what motivates them and for the secrets of their success. It is their own views only that we were interested in.

Do not look here, therefore, for an objective appraisal of any of the enterprises, nor for a 'how to succeed' guide to business or social venturing. This is a study of career choices, of the kind of experiences and influences that make someone into an alchemist, a person who makes a distinctive difference to the world around him or her. We hope that it will encourage more people to follow their example.

We did, however, look to see if there were any common threads or patterns in the different stories. If there are they will give leverage to the particular examples, suggesting that they are part of something bigger. In chapter one we have compared this set of individuals against three of the many theories and classifications that have been put forward in the area of creativity, innovation and entrepreneurship. Is it money, or power or something else that drives such people? In chapter two we look at the seeds of alchemy. Is it inherited? How much is luck and how much determination? Does it help to have a supportive family or is it a distraction? Does a good education help or hinder? Do you need a lot of money?

The quick answer to all these questions is 'Yes' and 'No'. There are, in our sample, no obvious determining conditions for alchemy and alchemists or, to put it another way, there are a lot of exceptions to every rule. This we believe to be important and exciting. It means that anyone can do it. The answer, for anyone interested, is to pick your model from the range on offer here to suit your own situation, ambitions and character.

Nevertheless, there were some features which were common enough to most of our alchemists to suggest that it would pay society to encourage them. Schooling, for instance, can often breed conformity rather than originality, which is why some of our sample chose to leave school as early as they could. The attitudes of parents in early childhood and adolescence can be critical. The full range of the possible implications for policy that arise from these examples will be discussed in more detail in chapter three.

Pictures often speak louder than words so this is, also, a book of portraits. The 'composite' portraits of our alchemists are intended to show more than one aspect of them or their work and to place them in their chosen context. These 'rounded' portraits repay study because they reveal almost as much about the individuals as the words they gave us. They also help us to identify with the person behind the list of achievements, people who are, to look at or to meet, no different from the rest of us.

About the Authors

Charles Handy is a writer, lecturer and broadcaster, a self-styled social philosopher and the author of books such as *The Empty Raincoat* and *The Hungry Spirit.*

Elizabeth Handy is a portrait photographer who has self-published two books of photography, *A Portrait of a Norfolk Village* and *A Journey Through Tea.*

Married for over thirty years, for the last ten of these they have combined their work in a close partnership, dividing the year between them so that each has priority for their own work during six months of the year, with the other acting in a supportive role.

This book, however, is their first joint project, for which Elizabeth provided the photographs and Charles the words. Both met every person featured in the book, talked with them together and shared their perceptions of the meetings.

They live in London and Norfolk. Norfolk is a rural retreat where they compose their portraits and their words, London their base for interaction with the world that they portray.

About the Photographs

Elizabeth Handy developed the style of 'joined' photography after studying the work of David Hockney and Christine Burrill.

Composing each portrait from up to twenty separate photographs she uses her camera like a paintbrush, emphasising some parts of the scene by duplication, suggesting movement in others, and capturing different images of the same person. Each portrait ends up with its own unique shape and offers the viewer an unusual glimpse into the subject's life.

The Nature of Alchemy

Each of the alchemists is very much his or her own person with a unique story, but if we want to see more such people in our society we need to know:

- what characteristics they may have in common (chapter one)
- what elements in their life stories helped to shape them (chapter two)

Only then can we go on to suggest how more people can be encouraged to go down the road of alchemy.

Twenty-nine individuals is a small sample. We therefore compared their stories with some other analyses of creative and entrepreneurial people. There are many such studies, but we turned in particular to three, each one very different in its approach but all concerned with originality, creativity and initiative. They are:

The Adventure Capitalists by Jeff Grout and Lynne Curry (Kogan Page, 1998), an account of conversations with twelve leading British business figures in 1994, including Sir Terence Conran who is also on our list.

Extraordinary Minds by Howard Gardner (Weidenfeld and Nicolson, 1997), an analysis of four exceptional people, Freud, Gandhi, Mozart and Virginia Woolf, and the lessons to be drawn from their creativity.

The Dynamics of Creation by Anthony Storr (Penguin, 1991), a psychiatrist's inquiry into why scientists and artists engage in creative activity, which Storr defines as 'the ability to bring something new into existence', very similar to our definition of an alchemist who creates something out of nothing.

Each of these studies looked at the problem from a different angle and used different concepts but, combined, they helped to explain a lot about our group.

THE COMMON CHARACTERISTICS OF ALCHEMISTS

These fall into three main groups which could be labelled Dedication, Doggedness and Difference.

1 *Dedication* Alternatively described in the books as 'commitment', 'drive', 'passion' or even 'obsession', it is clear that creativity and alchemy is not a chance affair. If you aren't dedicated to your enterprise, if you don't care passionately about what you are trying to bring about the chances are that it won't happen. Passion is not an extreme word for the way these alchemists felt about what they were doing. Many of them actually used the word, others talked of 'fascination', of 'the challenge' or of 'following their heart'. It was always clear, however, that what they were doing was central to their sense of themselves. To a large extent their work was them.

The dedication takes different forms. It can often be to the cause, particularly in the cases of people like Julia Middleton of Common Purpose, Andrew Mawson with the Bromley-by-Bow Centre or Sabrina Guinness of YCTV who have a particular social mission, or Rose Fenton and Lucy Neal who are determined to bring the best of foreign theatre to London via the London International Festival of Theatre and to involve London's schools in what they do.

Or it can be to the process. Terence Conran is passionate about design and quality in all aspects of life, just as Trevor Baylis cannot stop coming up with ideas for inventions that improve the lives of less fortunate people and is now dedicated to his idea of a potential academy for inventors to help others do likewise. Julian Richer, the founder of Richer Sounds, loves creating new and better businesses but is perhaps even more passionate today about his work in the voluntary sector. Martin

Leach, too, is passionate about each of his new publishing ventures, although he finds running them less exciting than starting them, so now plans to sell them on when established. When the passion goes so does the pleasure and, probably, the chances of continued success.

Tim Waterstone describes himself as passionate about marketing – books were the medium, much to his delight, but it could, he says, have been almost anything. Declan Donnellan and Nick Ormerod focus their dedication on the theatre, breathing new life into old masterpieces, and they knew from an early stage what it was that they wanted to do. So did Stephen Woodhams the landscape gardener, William Atkinson the teacher and many others. They are perhaps the lucky ones since they can get started early. Others stumble upon what will be their passion, like Ozwald Boateng whose early girlfriend got him sewing garments for her fashion show and so revealed to him his talent for tailoring.

Some kept their current dedication in abeyance while they got on with the rest of their life. Philip Hughes was a painter from early on but fitted it into his other career until he was ready to make it his full-time commitment. Jayesh Manek dabbled in investment on his own until twice winning a *Sunday Times* investment competition encouraged him to do it professionally. A hobby became a central passion. Trevor Baylis was a stunt swimmer, inventing things in his spare time until the inventions took over.

The dedication can emerge from sheer necessity. Dee Dawson created Britain's first and so far only specialist anorexic clinic because she was faced with a bankrupt husband and five young children, and had to find a way to live. Drawing on her business school education she looked for gaps in the health market. Anorexia was a neglected area of need at the time and so became the focus of her dedication but it did not begin that way. She now says that starting things will be her future passion.

Some people stumbled into it. Charles Dunstone was marking time before going to university by selling mobile phones for the Japanese electronic company NEC in the early days of the mobiles. He saw that he had landed in a new market and could get in at the beginning. Mapi Lucchesi would never be running her translation business had she not been sent to London from Tuscany to sell her uncle's cello, fallen in love with the place and come back to do the only thing she could at that time: translate languages.

Rarely, and never in our own list, was money itself the driving passion. Money is always a concern, of course, be the venture a business or a community initiative. 'We have to pay the bills,' says Richard Branson. In one sense a business has it easier because a successful one generates money, which can then be used to develop it. Even the promise of success can release money from backers. Community initiatives need money but do not generate money. They cannot, therefore, repay their backers in kind. Paradoxically, money is for them an even greater priority but, while always crucial, is never the driving purpose.

Some of our alchemists are rich, even very rich, but the wealth seems to be the score not the purpose. No one plays cricket for a batting average but a higher average is always welcomed by every cricketer as a mark of improvement. So it is for the business alchemists in our study. Richard Branson is pleased to be the largest privately owned business in Britain and his own wealth helps to fund his other enthusiasms, but the money, he claims, is not the point. Even in the artistic world, money seems to be the score, not the reason. Philip Hughes is pleased by the high prices his paintings fetch in the market, not because he needs the cash to spend but because the prices are one measure of his success as an artist. It is easier, of course, to take riches in your stride once you have them. For a struggling alchemist money is as much a necessity as a measure of success.

2 *Doggedness* Passion generates energy and the capacity for hard work. Just as well, because hard work, determination and tenacity are all needed. Prue Leith, another alchemist, although not in our sample, calls it doggedness. Dee Dawson said: 'Don't make it sound easy. It isn't.' Nevertheless, when it is your own creation that requires the effort it sometimes hardly seems like work. The answer to exhaustion is wholeheartedness, said a Benedictine monk. Tim Waterstone tells how he couldn't stay out of his bookstores in the first year or so. 'I kept popping in last thing before going home to see what was happening.' Work, Noël Coward said, can be more fun than fun – if it's that of your choice.

The alchemists have all laboured long hours, particularly in the early stages. Sometimes the nature of the work demands it. Stephen Woodhams, the landscape gardener, is at Covent Garden most mornings at 5 a.m. Richard Branson seems to be on the phone, working, wherever he is in the world. Sabrina Guinness is in the studio with the young television makers until late most evenings. So it seems to be with all the alchemists when the need arises.

It is tempting, in fact, to let the dedication to your creation absorb all the time available. That is when a passion becomes an obsession, something which can lead to distortions in both life and business. Anthony Storr points out that many of the world's great creators have been obsessives – Dickens, Stravinsky, Beethoven among them – or were manic-depressives including Michelangelo and Robert Schumann. We found no evidence of this, we are glad to say, in our sample. This may be because, unlike the examples quoted by Storr, our alchemists were not lonely creators; they all worked with others on their projects. Even Philip Hughes, the one artist among them, is also involved with the National Gallery – where he is Chairman of the Trustees – and is on the Board of a firm of publishers.

Some would admit, however, that the demands of the work and the long hours affected their home life. Ozwald Boateng and Tim Waterstone both thought that their concentration on their business in the early years might have contributed to the break-up of their marriages at that time. They have both now made a point of living differently. William Atkinson, the head teacher, feels that he did not see as much as he wished of his elder children when they were young and is determined to give enough time to the younger ones now.

Contrariwise, many on our list insist that their families provide stable centres in their lives and they are careful to make time for them. Jayesh Manek, the fund manager, is surrounded by his relatives at all times, living and working with members of his extended family and is convinced of its value to him in his work. Dennis Stevenson, an incredibly busy man with fingers in many pies, says his family is what matters most to him and arranges his time accordingly. Richard Branson may be on the phone everywhere but he takes his family away every school holiday and is careful to finish his phoning by midday on those days in order to give the rest of the day to his wife and teenage children.

Some, the women particularly, manage to combine hard work with large young families. Both Julia Middleton and Dee Dawson have five children. Lucy Neal has four and her partner, Rose, has two. They have to be very disciplined in organizing their time, and need to work extremely efficiently. Mapi Lucchesi has a new-born baby to feed every few hours but takes her work home to do it, using her computer with the baby on her arm. They are all living proof that you can combine family responsibilities with the management of demanding organizations – as long as you are in control of your own schedule.

Eight of the alchemists are single. The temptation then is even greater to let your enthusiasm for your work take over everything else. They all, however, insist that there has to be another dimension to life and that you have to plan it in. John McLaren is not only a banker and a lover of music but also writes novels in his holidays. Stephen Woodhams loves travel and uses his business opportunities to get where he wants to go. Like Martin Leach, the publisher, they are all careful to take short but frequent holidays and to discipline their work life. Sabrina Guinness, although passionate about her involvement with the young people in her television studio, delights in leaving it all behind of an evening and going out to a different world. Charles Dunstone and Trevor Baylis both make sure that there is enough time for the boats they love.

Doggedness also includes what the poet Keats called *negative capability*: the capacity to keep going when things are going wrong, or when you are in the midst of doubts and uncertainties. You can only demonstrate this, however, if you feel convinced of the worth of what you are doing, if you believe in yourself and have the courage and patience to ride out the storms. Some alchemists – Dee Dawson, for instance – take discouragement as a challenge. Tell her that she can't do something and her blood is up. William Atkinson received over fifty rejections in his search for a deputy head's post in a school but persisted and eventually succeeded. Trevor Baylis had his idea of a clockwork radio scorned by everyone he showed it to, but he persevered, with sheer doggedness, until BayGen heard of it and bought the rights to make it in South Africa.

Almost all the alchemists have had to face failure of one sort or another and to get over it. Creativity is not guaranteed to work all the time. Risk is risky because things go wrong. The true alchemists manage to twist it round. They talk of their mistakes or failures as learning experiences. Ozwald Boateng, made bankrupt by the cancellation of some big Far Eastern orders, was back in business a week later, resolved this time to take more interest in the finances of his tailoring company. Richard Branson is still sad that he had to sell his music business to finance his airline, weeping when he saw the headline of the sale in the evening paper, but it made him realize that he was foolish ever to let himself become beholden to bankers or, later, to outside shareholders.

Some upsets can even be the start of alchemy, revealing not who we are but who we almost certainly are not. Dennis Stevenson was destined for an academic career until an unexpected set-back in his final examinations sent him looking for an opening in business instead. No doubt he would have been a good academic but we would have missed his career of serial alchemy in high places. Martin Leach was set for a future in the travel industry until financial disaster sent him looking for work in publishing and the realization that he could do better himself what other people were paying him to do for them. The message is that every set-back is almost always an opportunity in disguise but to see it you have to have both self-belief and negative capability. Anthony Storr points out that the ability to tolerate tension and anxiety is characteristic of the creative person.

3 *Difference* Passion and doggedness, however, are not enough in themselves. Bull-headed bullies may be dogged and passionate but remain rigid enforcers of the *status quo*. There has to be something else that makes an alchemist: a mixture, it seems, of both personality and talent. We have labelled it 'difference'.

All the alchemists say that they want to make a difference, in some way, somehow. To do that they have to do things differently or do different things, maybe even themselves be different from the rest of us. Some of our sample started off different, as outsiders in one way or another. Martin Leach came to London from New Zealand, Mapi Lucchesi from Italy, both of them knowing no one. Ozwald Boateng arrived in traditional Savile Row as an outsider, young, Ghanaian and bold in his designs. It may be tough at first but outsiders can't be classified. They are free to break the norms without criticism; they are accepted as different from the start.

Creative people, other research suggests, like to cultivate their difference, by which they mean their particular edge or talent, while the rest of us are still wondering what is different about ourselves, what talent we can lay claim to. Some of us even hope that we aren't, that we can fit the norms we see around us and conform to other people's expectations. The cultivation of one's particular difference, one's uniqueness, is in many ways the secret to success in life for all of us but alchemists do it better because they do it with both dedication and doggedness. Some creatives, in fact, seem to delight in difference of all sorts, to the point of being defined as mavericks or rebels in early life.

This is true of many of our group, even if they are now careful to clothe their maverick instincts in more conventional garb. If you want to change things, the saying goes, wear a dark suit when you preach radical thoughts. Michael Young is a determined revolutionary, founding nearly fifty reforming institutions in his long life, but he has always been the reasonable face of radical ideas and long ago accepted a seat in the House of Lords. Julia Middleton inherited, she says, her father's rebellious streak, but has successfully wooed the Establishment in pursuit of her passion for her educational venture, Common Purpose. In Virgin, Richard Branson has even made a brand out of being both different and maverick and so made difference respectable.

None of our group would fit easily into the ranks of a large organization. They would be very uncomfortable subordinates, since their delight in difference makes them intolerant of both conformity and assumed authority. They start enterprises and run them but they don't work their way up them. The one-time organization man, Tim Waterstone, was eventually sacked. 'I thought that I could do things better than them,' he says. Charles Dunstone lasted one year at NEC before thinking similar thoughts and launching Carphone Warehouse for himself. Martin Leach was told that he was unemployable. Dennis Stevenson today inhabits huge organizations but enters only at the top. Robert Ayling, having been a lawyer and civil servant before joining British Airways, is perhaps an exception, although he, too, came in at the top, where making a difference is often the point of the job.

If you don't like bosses, or organizations unless they are the ones you yourself created, then you will almost inevitably be seen as controlling. Control seems to be a necessary consequence of turning difference into alchemy. Having done it your way so successfully it can be hard to let go. Although they hide it behind a modest demeanour, all the alchemists clearly needed to be in control, even if much of the day-to-day responsibility was delegated. The commercial ones were reluctant to take their businesses public because, as Richard Branson and Terence Conran both found out, you lose a lot of control over your future.

All the newly founded organizations, whether in business or in the non-profit sector, could be described as an extension of the person of the founder. Many said that part of the joy of their work was the chance to do it with people they liked. This is another way of saying that they were staffing the place with complementary extensions of themselves. This is both natural and probably right as a management strategy. It makes the place feel like a family and is a recognized feature of successful small family businesses. It emphasizes the personality of the alchemist, which then infects the organization.

It can, however, be dangerous if the personality at the centre is not open to criticism or fresh ideas. Alchemy then withers because no one person can be the fount of all the creativity needed by a growing enterprise. Our alchemists seemed different. They delighted, they insisted, in new ideas and constructive feedback. Julian Richer credits his suggestions schemes with much of the success of his companies and, through his foundation, funds the innovative charity projects that his work-force comes up with. If the claims of our alchemists are true they reinforce the finding from other research that creatives are, by nature, different from the bulk of managers in that they are both self-promoting and, at the same time, self-questioning. Decent Doubt and Confident Certainty are both necessary for effective alchemy, although they make uneasy partners and can result in confusing messages.

This aspect of difference is not surprising if one looks at other research on creative people. This research has found that creatives tend to reject the simple and the already completed in favour of the complicated and unfinished but then want to apply their own solutions. This preference is statistically connected with independence, originality, verbal fluency, breadth of interests, impulsiveness and expansiveness. It is negatively correlated with conservatism, control of impulse, social conformity and rigidity. Many creatives were observed to be happy only when working on a new problem and required recurrent challenges as a stimulus. Our interviews broadly support these findings.

Successful alchemists find the way through their challenges with what Grout and Curry have called the 'third eye'. This is the ability to look at things from a different angle, to stand outside the mental box in which many imprison themselves. Behind the third eye is an endless curiosity that asks 'why?' and 'why not?' in apparently ordinary situations. The young Terence Conran found chefs in Paris frustrating and authoritarian so decided that what was needed was a restaurant without chefs and the Soup Kitchen was born. Rose Fenton and Lucy Neal felt that London Theatre was too parochial so decided to start a biennial International Festival of Theatre on their own.

The examples go on. John McClaren deplored the way that classical music was heading therefore, although heavily engaged in his work as a merchant banker, sensed that a competition for new composers, which guaranteed worldwide audiences to the winners would rejuvenate the genre and so founded Masterprize. Dennis Stevenson looked at a redundant power station on the Thames in London and saw, with his third eye, a new museum of modern art. Trevor Baylis watched a television programme on AIDS in Africa and saw how a simple clockwork mechanism could bring portable radios to African villages. Declan Donnellan looked at his actors with a third eye and sensed new possibilities in their performances. Jane Tewson says that she comes in 'off the beam' in meetings, 'which people seem to value'. In one way or another all our alchemists have demonstrated the use of that third eye.

Alchemists may be different in yet another way. One observation reported by psychologists testing male creative persons is that they show high scores on scales measuring 'femininity'. 'The evidence is clear', says one report. 'The more creative a person is the more he [*sic*] reveals an openness to his own feelings and emotions, a sensitive intellect and understanding self-awareness. Our creative subjects appear to give more expression to the feminine side of their nature than do less creative persons.' Whether creative women show more masculine interests than average is not so well established, but Anthony Storr quotes anecdotal evidence to suggest that it might be so. It is a truism that we all have both male and female parts to our psyche but perhaps alchemists have a more equal balance of the two sexes than most of us.

We did not inquire specifically into this question in our interviews but we were impressed by the intuitive and self-aware attitude of our male interviewees and by the forceful approach to their work of our female subjects. If these are aspects of the male and female components of our personalities then we can probably say that alchemists are more truly bisexual in personality than the average person. It was interesting that, more than would be usual, the men quoted their mothers as the dominant influences in their childhoods, while for many of the women it was their fathers. This would explain how so many of both sexes end up with both the third eye and the forcefulness to put the insights to work. Alchemy needs both to be more than wistful dreaming.

4 *In Summary*   Some truths need resurrection rather than discovery. Writing about genius in the mid-nineteenth century, Francis Galton said that three things were necessary for great achievement – 'ability', 'zeal' and 'a capacity for hard work'. Maybe we have only demonstrated that these things are still true today and have relabelled them 'difference', 'dedication' and 'doggedness'.

We have wondered, however, about the motivation of our alchemists. What is it that drives them? Money, power and fame were possibilities. It is our strong feeling that none of these is the driving force. Money is necessary. It can also be the measure of success, but measures, we have argued, are not the same as purposes.

Power, or control, is also essential, at least in the early stages, and often seems to be a part of the alchemist personality, but we do not feel that the urge to control in this group reaches further than their own creations. They don't hanker after political power, nor do they want to build huge corporations. None of them is an aspiring Rupert Murdoch.

Fame, like money, might be the result of successful alchemy, might even be cultivated in order to promote alchemy, but is not itself, we feel, the motivating force for the people we met. Some had had honours thrust upon them but others resist the very idea of public recognition as a diversion from their mission. Nevertheless, they all want to be successful. These people are high achievers, although they claim to be ambitious for their projects more than for themselves. They are never satisfied, always looking for new mountains to climb, forever competing with themselves. 'I am still pregnant,' says William Atkinson, the head teacher, as he contemplates his future.

We are left with something that other research into creativity has suggested as part of the make-up of the creative personality – the urge to express oneself. Why else do artists paint or poets write their intimate thoughts? Why do writers write when most must know that few will read their books unless they are very fortunate? Without a creative project this expressive urge can take the form of excessive egotism, of narcissism or even violence and criminality. What alchemists do is to take this urge and turn it into something, be it a business, a piece of theatre, a project, a building or a work of art, a reborn school or a think tank. They turn their different talents into passions and apply doggedness until they bear fruit. If the result then shows some of the hallmarks of their personality that is both understandable and forgivable.

The Seeds of Alchemy

Perhaps we are all alchemists at heart. If so, we need to know what makes it real for some and not for others. What makes an alchemist? We looked at three aspects of the life of our sample to see if we could find any common clues: early childhood, education and critical events.

1 *Early Childhood* Some things we can't do anything about: our genes, for instance. There is no doubt that many of the special talents or aptitudes of a few of our alchemists owe something to previous generations of their families. Conran's mother was, he is sure, a talented designer who never practised because the culture of the times did not favour middle-class wives developing their own careers. Boateng's was a seamstress, so he should not have been so surprised that he was good at tailoring. Stephen Woodhams feels that he was destined to be a gardener by profession when he learnt that his grandfather was one. Geoff Mulgan tells how he looked up the name Mulgan on the Internet and discovered that all the individuals listed there, and probably related to him, were involved in social action, as was he.

On the other hand, many could trace no history of their enthusiasms or talents in their families. Genes don't define the whole of our lives. Nor does birth order, although it started as a tempting hypothesis when the first six people we interviewed were second children. The hypothesis was that first-born children would be more conformist. They might be equally successful but in a more conventional way. The second or third, with fewer expectations loaded on to him or her, would be more free to be different. In the final count, twenty are second or third in line, well over half but not quite enough to prove a rule. What matters is what lies behind the birth order – the attitude and expectations of parents.

Ozwald Boateng was the third child of Ghanaian parents living in London. His father – and unusually for this group it was the father not the mother – made it clear to him from an early age that he was expected to be successful, in fact *the* successful one of the family. They all knew this and have always rallied behind Ozwald. This sort of expectation more normally went with the first-born and Ozwald might well have responded by adopting a very orthodox career. Instead, he interpreted it as an invitation to shape his own destiny, and quickly. Richard Branson, on the other hand, was the first child. His parents, too, expected much, but more by way of character and independence of spirit than conventional success. Both sets of parents backed their sons when life became difficult and both acquiesced in their leaving education as soon as they could. Joanne McFarlane was very conscious of her parents' high expectations for her and, like several others, was pleased to be able to share her success with them. The hope that one's parents will be proud of one's achievements is often part of our motivation. 'My father finally understood what I was doing and was impressed,' said Mapi Lucchesi thankfully.

Some, however, found that their parents had little or no expectations for them. William Atkinson, Michael Young, Mapi Lucchesi, Sabrina Guinness, Dee Dawson and Martin Leach came from very different sorts of families. They were, however, all ones where parents either didn't care much what their kids did in life or else only wanted them to follow convention, marry and have children of their own. For these individuals it was essential to escape the parental influences if they were to flourish as their instincts told them they might. Families, current research deliberates, don't matter as much as the peer group. Our interviews suggest that strong parents and secure homes do matter. Most of our alchemists come from stable, happy families. It is when the parents fail to exercise their influence or to care that other groups and persons become important.

Jean-Paul Sartre said that the best thing a father could do for his children was to die young. There is much anecdotal evidence that the early death or departure of a father forces the son to take on responsibility and to mature more quickly. Many American presidents, including

Clinton, had lost their fathers before the age of fourteen. Sixty-one per cent of British prime ministers between 1803 and 1941 had lost a parent early in life. There is no evidence to support this possibility in our sample. No fathers died young, although some, like William Atkinson's, were notably absent. That may be a statistical accident of this sample. On the other hand enforced early maturity may hinder future creativity even if it stimulates responsibility and a desire to achieve. Creativity, to be productive, needs both the curiosity and inventiveness of the child, and the responsibility and focus of the adult. One without the other won't result in alchemy. In other words such premature deaths do not usually result in alchemists, even if they do produce an unusual proportion of presidents, prime ministers and high achievers.

Genes or no genes, parents and other close relatives provide role models, whether they intend to or not. Rose Fenton's parents led a very unconventional life, carting their children around Europe in a van for six months at a time when they should have been at school. Feeling embarrassed at first because of living such a different life from her young school mates, Rose came to realize that she was envied for her eccentric parents and life-style. From then on 'different' was acceptable to Rose, even desirable. What you can't predict, of course, is whether your children will accept your unconscious role modelling or reject it. Mapi Lucchesi deliberately rejected that of her mother and most of the others chose not to follow their parents' more structured careers. It may be that their children, in turn, will reject the alchemist model. All that parents can do, if they want to influence their children's lives, is to be aware that they and teachers are often the only live models their children have on which to base their ideas about adult life. If they appear unsatisfactory the children will look elsewhere.

Research into the early lives of expatriate executives has shown that where the children were exposed to a range of different experiences, homes, or countries in their youth and prospered because they felt secure and loved, then when adult they implicitly accepted that change could be beneficial and pleasant. Secure childhoods don't have to be static. Early exposure to different environments, as several of our sample experienced when their parents moved location, can be a good preparation for a changing world, provided that one is surrounded by love. John McLaren moved a lot as his father changed his postings but recalls no problems or anguish. Jayesh Manek was sent from Uganda to school in England by his parents when only fifteen but knew for sure that his elder brothers would be there to help should he need them. He has never since been fearful of breaking out on his own.

Early responsibility and accountability is a useful start to independence, if the parents can stand it. For many in the sample alchemy began young, particularly among those destined to be business entrepreneurs. Richard Branson was starting a Christmas tree farm in the field behind the house, and a budgie-breeding business while at school. Both failed, but that didn't matter, the urge was not discouraged by his parents. Julian Richer and Ozwald Boateng were traders at school. Mapi Lucchesi, aged eight, sold white pebbles in her village and hired out her good-looking brother as a film extra. Stephen Woodhams sold vegetables from his greenhouse to his teachers at secondary school. On another front, Geoff Mulgan was a social activist, raising money and leading local protest groups in his early teens.

2 *Education* Adolescence is the main period of identity formation. A large part of this time is spent in education and at school. School, therefore, inevitably fashions our early impressions of what the world outside the family will be like and what our role will be in it. It is, however, the process of education as much as the content that shapes our future lives. A highly regimented and authoritarian school will not offer much space or encouragement for anyone who wants to be different. At the other extreme, Michael Young found the freedom of Dartington School a sort of heaven after the trials of his earlier years and a huge encouragement to develop his own very different identity, and Jane Tewson, after one very traditional school proved unsympathetic to her dyslexic problems, discovered a new self-confidence and creativity in her local comprehensive, which allowed her to be herself.

For others the school regime remained too restricted and formalized. Almost half of them left at sixteen or eighteen, sometimes returning later to formal education. School, as they experienced it, did not value their differences. Those who stayed did so, either because they found scholastic work easy and the companionship enjoyable, or because they were lucky enough to meet a teacher who valued their difference and fortified their self-belief.

Julian Richer is now proud to be the youngest governor of his school where he was a poor student but where he started his commercial career by selling hi-fi equipment with the quiet support of his teacher. Without that he might well have left. Richard Branson did leave, in a hurry to promote his first big venture, his Student magazine. Ozwald Boateng was another who practised commerce at school, this time selling videos not hi-fi. He left as soon as he could to start being different outside. Joanne McFarlane's school, where she was the only black person in her year, tried hard to ignore her and made her life miserable. She departed and subsequently blossomed in her college.

Overall, however, great teachers come out well in our study. Terence Conran was lucky to meet up with some of Britain's greatest craftsmen at Bryanston in the war years where, as conscientious objectors, they were teaching instead of fighting. Dennis Stevenson and Andy Law both encountered inspiring teachers at their schools. William Atkinson, who started secondary school with the unusual distinction of having failed his Eleven Plus examination twice (because they at first confused him with his elder brother) met a great teacher when he finally made it to the sixth form, a person who gave him his love of education. Michael Young's young life was transformed by the Elmhirsts at Dartington. All these teachers, and some others, made their students confident in their differences.

Other studies have suggested that too much schooling for too long can dent or suppress creativity. Ours indicates that it depends on the schooling. Where 'otherness' is not only tolerated but built upon, where there is enough cultural space to be different, where teachers have the time and the willingness to act as mentors, tuition can help the individual to leverage that difference, by, for instance, also winning the grades that are the passports to both more education and to other areas of life later on. It is interesting, however, that even those whose education was trouble free and scholastically successful mentioned it as important only if they had encountered in the course of it some imaginative individual teacher. Everything in the experiences of our sample reinforces the research that suggests that IQ has no correlation with creativity. You can be creative *and* clever, in the conventional sense, or creative and the school dunce.

Schools are the first experience that any young person has of an organization other than the family. They therefore fix the mind-set that the young adult will carry into the world of work. If the school is authoritarian, regimented and regulated, the young person is likely to assume that all organizations are like that, with no room for uniqueness, with success measured clinically by grades and examinations, and creativity outside the art class defined as disruptive behaviour. The implication then is that to be creative one has to operate outside traditional set-ups or create your own. No wonder some would-be alchemists leave early. Does that matter? Probably not. You can always learn what you need to later. Ozwald Boateng went off to a business course when he realized that great tailoring was not enough to make a successful tailoring company.

On the other hand we don't know, and will never know, how many potential alchemists have been squashed in the bud by over-regimented schools, with their disciplined regime reinforced by conformist parents. As with all this research, we could only study what we saw, not what might have been.

3 *Critical Events and Persons*   'Follow your heart and grab your luck,' is Sabrina Guinness's advice to aspiring alchemists. Almost all the people whom we have interviewed for this book say that they had been lucky at some stage in their lives. We make our own luck to an extent. More accurately, we open ourselves to it. We go to the orchards where the apples are ripe so that when one falls we are there and ready to catch it. Some even shake the trees. Those who visit no orchards catch no apples. 'Lucky' people see opportunities where others observe nothing unusual. It is the third eye at work. 'Lucky' individuals fasten on to people or situations that can help them. They literally do grab their good fortune as Sabrina herself did when accidentally meeting Ryan O'Neal playing fris-

bee in a London park in her late teens. He asked her to go to Los Angeles for six months as nanny to his daughter. She went and it changed her life. There were a dozen other young women in the group that afternoon but only Sabrina engaged with Ryan. She made her own luck.

None of these people planned his or her career. 'Take your work seriously but improvise your career,' advises Declan Donnellan, which is what he has always done. After closing down his theatre company Cheek by Jowl, his future looked uncertain, but nine months later he was in Moscow receiving a national award, unprecedented for a non-Russian, for Best Production for his version of *The Winter's Tale* in Russian at the Maly Theatre in St Petersburg. Improvisation means snatching opportunities. For nearly all our sample there was a critical event that posed a choice. They could have ignored the opportunity but by taking the adventurous route and choosing 'the road less travelled' they changed the course of their lives.

Geoff Mulgan, aged twenty-eight at the time, had accepted a job in the European Commission in Brussels, one offering all the potential of an international civil service career with a great salary and benefits. The week before he was due to go Gordon Brown, now the Chancellor of the Exchequer but then in opposition, asked him to come and run his office – much less pay, no career prospects, but far more intriguing. Geoff accepted and never went to Brussels. 'That call changed my life,' he says. 'If it had come a week later I could not have accepted.' It was a chance to be snatched, not a planned career move. To plan can be to blinker oneself, screening out other opportunities.

Dennis Stevenson, aged twenty-five, wrote to Peter Walker, then a Cabinet minister, suggesting that a bill going through Parliament aimed at regulating pop festivals was dangerously draconian. Peter Walker thereupon invited him to draw up a code of practice for pop festivals, of which Dennis knew little, and offered him a small team of civil servants to assist him. Dennis accepted, but he didn't have to. Walker then asked him to become Chairman of a New Town corporation, one in the northeast of England full of out-of-work miners. It was an unprecedented offer to a young man with no experience. Dennis had a business to run in London. He had every reason to turn it down. He didn't and made his name. He was fortunate, yes, but he engineered his luck and took his opportunity with both hands.

Declan Donnellan and Nick Ormerod were lucky to meet Lyall Jones at the start of their theatre career. He saw a production they had put on in a pub with actors performing for free and invited them to direct his students at the Arts Education Drama School. It was their breakthrough. It was there that Declan initially developed his style of directing and it led to their first Arts Council tour. They were lucky that Lyall Jones came to see their performance but they, penurious young men, had made the luck possible by persuading some successful actors to work with them for nothing in a very speculative venture.

Andy Law experienced what seemed at first to be a bit of bad luck. The advertising agency that he ran in London was sold over his head by the parent company in America. It was a critical time. He was thirty-eight with a growing family. He could go on working as a rich slave for his new bosses or he could do things his own way. He persuaded his colleagues to leave and start their own innovative agency. It was risky, of course, but it was his chance to run an organization the way he thought it could be run and to test his beliefs. He was lucky, he says, to have had the chance, but he grabbed the opportunity where many others would have sighed and done nothing.

Philip Hughes had bought a book on computing, a new topic in the early Sixties, when, passing a shop window, he saw that the premises were the front office of a software consulting company, one of the first of its kind. He went in and got a job. He calls it chance, but his eyes were open for it. When Julian Richer went to rent his first shop, the landlord not only rented it to him without a premium but gave him a £20,000 loan in return for the option to buy a chunk of the equity. Chance? Or was Julian astute enough to sell his vision while asking for a lease?

For some, the critical events have been problems which turned out to be opportunities. Terence Conran could not sell the new-look furniture that he was manufacturing. He went to look at the retail showrooms. They were displaying his furniture amid the stacks of mock antiques and garish suites where it looked horribly out of place. He realized that if his designs were going to sell he would have to open his own retail store. So Habitat was born, as was Conran's continuing fascination with the retail end of things. Richard Branson, asked for the rationale behind his multifarious range of businesses, from airlines to pensions to mobile phones, replies that he turns his frustrations into businesses. Fed up with poor service on the planes he travelled on, he resolved to see if he could do better and the result was Virgin Atlantic.

The message that comes through from all the stories is one of seizing chances, of turning problems into opportunities, of using one's luck. 'Believe in fate,' said the actress Lesley Joseph once. 'But lean forward so that fate can see you.' That requires self-confidence and self-belief, and a bit of cheek at times. That nugget of self-belief came early to nearly all in our sample. The parents of most were encouraging at the beginning, but that is expected of parents by their children. Real reinforcement has to come from someone else.

For many it was a teacher. Praise from respected adults always helps. Dennis Stevenson had two 'brilliant' teachers who assured him that he, too, could be brilliant. Dee Dawson had one 'fantastic' teacher in biology. 'I got the top grade in biology for the whole examining board. He was very pleased by that. Then I knew I wasn't stupid.' Stephen Woodhams was inspired by the apprentice masters he met at the Royal College of Horticulture. For others it came later. Andrew Mawson's 'critical figures' were John Shaw, a Methodist minister who got him interested in the 'why' questions and encouraged him to return to education, and, later, Eric Blakeborough who became a powerful role model for him.

Mentors and role models were important for almost everyone. They give confidence and radiate reassurance. Julia Middleton speaks of her early bosses, John Garnett, Julia Cleverdon and Rupert Middleton, as powerful influences. Tim Waterstone, likewise, nominates Derrick Holden-Brown, the head of his first employer, as a powerful influence. For Robert Ayling it was his wife Julia and her architect father, who taught him to understand space, something which was to be crucial when commissioning his visionary new offices. For Geoff Mulgan it may have been a German monk in Sri Lanka during his gap year before university who inspired him.

41

Mentors cannot be imposed. They happen, and it requires a certain chemistry for the mentoring process to work. The alchemists are unusual in their eagerness to look for them and to learn from them. This is perhaps the self-confidence that comes from knowing what you want to do even if you don't always know how to get there, the mixture of decent doubt and confident certainty that we earlier identified as one of the characteristics of alchemy. 'You build mountains for yourself to climb,' grumbled Dee Dawson's mother, but that, in the end, is what all the alchemists do and wise mountaineers are never ashamed to take a guide with them.

4 *In Conclusion*   Creativity and curiosity are part of the human condition. We all have them to some degree. They are, however, easily stifled. Declan Donnellan maintains that curiosity is the more important of the two, because if you know what the 'why?' questions are it is not that difficult to find some possible answers.

The alchemists in our group managed to get through early childhood and education without losing that curiosity. In some cases it was encouraged, in some stimulated. Some escaped before it was squashed. In some it was clearly irrepressible. Curiosity is, however, a tender flower. So is self-esteem, the crucial bit that is necessary to advance from curiosity to creativity. They both need nurturing. Once again, we shall never know how many alchemists there might have been had their curiosity not been crushed in their youth, or called impertinence, and their self-confidence dented because mistakes were too often branded failures, or because self-expression by the young was deemed by their elders to be inappropriate if not arrogant. Discipline needs to be tempered with tolerance and freedom or licence balanced with a respect for others. The next chapter discusses how this might be done better in our societies.

Growing More Alchemists

'Entrepreneurs aren't born, they happen,' says Dennis Stevenson. We have seen some evidence of how they happen. Must we then just wait for them to occur by chance or can we change any of the conditions in society to encourage more of them? If curiosity and creativity are indeed part of our human condition, why is it that there aren't more alchemists already? After talking with the people in our study it is our belief that the happening need not be left to chance. It can and should be influenced.

Some will argue that it would be an anarchic world if everyone practised alchemy. Of course. There have to be those who maintain institutions as well as those who create them. We need many who are content with the mundane and are happy to work to a routine, as well as those who like to be told what to do rather than to invent it. Entrepreneurial bus drivers or air traffic controllers are only needed in dire emergencies. Alchemy should have no place in a well-ordered organization or society, say some; or, at least, it should know its place, which is in the research and artistic institutions.

Nevertheless, without alchemy we would stagnate. No one wants to live in a world that is frozen in time. A nation would rapidly become impoverished if it tried to live only on the products and services of its past. The same is true of its social institutions. Andrew Mawson, one of our alchemists, is spearheading a drive to find 2000 social entrepreneurs by the year 2000. Michael Young, another alchemist, has founded a School for Social Entrepreneurs in order to boost the supply of such people.

Unfortunately it cannot always be that easy. Creativity in harness can turn uncreative. Alchemy is unruly, it leaps boundaries, breaks out of boxes, defies conventions. Nor can it be sure to work. There are thought to be ten bad ideas for every good one, although since few

43

admit to the bad ones no one can prove this hypothesis. Alchemy, there-fore, is wasteful as well as unpredictable. Crick and Watson, the discov-ers of DNA, perhaps the most significant scientific step forward in this century, would never, they say, have come upon it had they not been given the money, by the Science Research Council, to let their imagina-tions flow free in Cambridge with no preformed expectations of the out-come. Alchemy, it would seem, needs a culture of experimentation, not of control, if it is to happen.

It is a tough dilemma for a place like Singapore, which is concerned to develop more local creative and entrepreneurial talent. Hitherto focused on doing better what the Western countries already do, Singapore now needs to be different as well as better if she is to continue her record of growth into the next millennium. Can such a regulated society grow alchemists? is the question that they are asking them-selves. How might they deliberately foster more such people without the alchemy spreading unrest in the streets? It is a problem not unique to Singapore but one that faces governments and corporations every-where. Corporations instinctively dislike things that are out of control or can't be planned and counted. Their hearts shudder at the thought of the slack or waste that comes with too much experimentation even though their minds tell them that it is essential. The uncomfortable truth is that alchemy and controlled efficiency don't go well together.

There are many reports and studies on entrepreneurship and the ways to encourage more of it. It is not our purpose to comment on these studies but rather to emphasize the ideas which stem directly from our interviews.

Twenty-nine people is too small a sample to be significant as a basis for policy. Nevertheless, the studies in this book do throw up a number of ideas for consideration. Drawing on the last two chapters we have grouped these ideas under two headings – '*Zeitgeist*' and 'Formation', both words foreign in their origin, suggesting that the concepts behind them may be alien to the English, who have a long-established reputa-tion for creating ideas that someone else then develops. If this sort of aborted alchemy really is a trademark of the English, perhaps it has something to do with the two headings that we have identified.

1 *Zeitgeist*   There was, we suggested earlier, something in the air in Florence in the fifteenth century and in Athens two thousand years before that. It didn't last for ever but at its peak those cities attracted and bred great innovators in the arts, philosophy, government and warfare. These people fed off each other. So it may be with Dublin today, the city at the heart of the Irish renaissance, a time when Irish theatre and music, as much as business, is having a heyday. Clusters, a concept developed to explain business success stories, may well apply equally well to creativity and alchemy. A clustering of the arts, new young companies, a population of young people, good educational facilities, research institutes, future-orientated bankers and liberal lawmakers, these seem to infect each other and to provide models for others to imitate.

Florence had all of these elements. So, in its own time, did Athens. Boston and the Bay Area in California have them in America. We believe that London has most of them today. Berlin may well be the next clustering complex, bringing a new wave of alchemy to Germany. By contrast Singapore, a city of almost four million people, has no professional theatre company or orchestra, its universities, although good at what they do, are teaching institutions not research bases, while their bankers are lenders rather than venturers. Nor does it help that the best of their young often leave the country for further education and do not return. As a result the requisite clustering for alchemy is not yet there, although the government, far-sighted if at this time not noticeably liberal, is working to create it with a new arts centre under construction, research bases beginning to be established at the universities and leading scientists brought in to kick-start them. There is a fresh emphasis on creativity in the schools and a campaign to attract creative young Asians to make their base in Singapore.

The examples cited are all cities. This seems to be a phenomenon of cities and their surrounding hinterland. Proximity breeds infection and osmosis. Alchemy thrives on both. There is a velocity of ideas in a place like Silicon Valley that can be intoxicating to those caught up in it, releasing energies and creativity that they were often unaware of. National governments can help or hinder with their policies on taxation, subsidy and general economic measures but for the most part it is up to individual cities to create the requisite *Zeitgeist* or mood. Most reports stress the need for risk money, and venture capital as the essential pre-conditions of entrepreneurship, but cash, strangely perhaps, is not the real problem at the start, neither for the participants in our study nor for most entrepreneurs. The average business entrepreneur, in both Britain and America, starts with less than £10,000, from personal savings or from a family loan. It is at the next stage that serious funds are needed, to finance the first stage of expansion.

It is not, therefore, the availability of finance that attracts alchemists in the first place. Creative people flock where creative things are happening; where mavericks congregate, irreverence thrives and disrespect for convention and authority is accepted. The arts which, at their best, connect the unconnected, along with the research side of higher education, are the easiest places to start injecting some of this requisite alchemy. If the educational facilities are good and the arts are thriving, industry will start to follow, in search of talent and ideas. Money follows business and where there is ready cash life picks up, with stores, restaurants and a demand for services, all of which offer easy opportunities for small-scale alchemy.

Dundee, a dour town in the east of Scotland noted in the past for jam and jute, is seeking to reinvent itself. It has become one of the world's fastest-growing bio-technology centres, with heavy investments made in medical and genetic research. There is a growing university population and, equally important, an increased arts budget with an impressive new cultural centre of spacious galleries and auditoriums, a thriving repertory company and community drama programme, splendid dance studios all topped off by a slogan proclaiming itself as the City of Discovery. It may prove to be too small to become a real cluster of alchemy but it is certainly going the right way about it.

We need more Dundees if our societies are going to be places of what Adam Smith, the first high priest of the market economy, said should be our real aim in society, namely 'cultivation'. Ironically, in this new age of knowledge and ideas, economies won't grow without a base of cultivation, just as cultivation won't survive without a good economy. They are necessary bedfellows, both dependent on successful alchemists. This, ultimately, is the justification for subsidy to the arts, although calling it a subsidy undermines it. Investment would be a better word, just as we don't talk about subsidizing education or even, in Britain, of subsidizing industry when we do it, calling it instead an investment grant to foster local employment. Investment for alchemy is long-term, unpredictable, wasteful at times. It requires governments who can look beyond the grave and certainly beyond the next election.

2 *Formation*   The French speak of 'formation' when referring to the whole development of a professional person. Having originally borrowed the word entrepreneur from them we should be well advised to take over their concept of formation because it goes beyond what happens in and around the classroom to include all the formative influences on a person. Alchemists are formed rather than educated, although formal education has its part to play. We make a great mistake if we believe that what happens in school is the main determinant of our future. Any quick reading of the stories in this book should be enough to dissuade one from that idea.

Childhood experiences, wherever they occur, establish patterns of thought and behaviour which form deep roots. Early responsibility as a small child, the chance to test one's curiosity by experiment, to learn that mistakes are not fatal and that change can be exciting, these are the initial seeds of alchemy – stifle them and you risk stunting the creative potential of the young child. Unfortunately, fearful of the dangers of modern society, children today are often over-cosseted, particularly in big cities. Ferried everywhere in cars or buses, guarded from strangers, prevented even from playing with friends in case they are hurt and sue their hosts, there is often nothing left to experimental youngsters except computer games in the security of their own homes.

A 1999 BBC study of 1300 young people found that they were fed up with being corralled and over-supervised by parents and teachers. *Bright Futures,* a report form the Mental Health Foundation, makes the same point: 'As a result of parental fears there appears to have been a dramatic decrease in both the range of unaccompanied activities undertaken by children and the amount of interaction between children and adults.'

We have to find a way to create more safe but experimental opportunities for the next generation.

We also need to embrace the ideas of two Americans, Howard Gardner and Daniel Goleman, and their concepts of intelligence or, as we would rather call it, of talent. We have already commented on the fact that IQ, the conventional measurement of intelligence, seems to have no correlation with creativity. There was one famous study, by Lewis Terman, of high IQ children in California who grew up in the early years of the century and were followed throughout their lives. They were successful and happy, but none of them was noticeably creative – there were no writers or artists, no scientists of note.

Gardner and Goleman go a long way to explaining why. They redefine intelligence to mean much more than the aspects of it measured by IQ tests. Call it talent rather than intelligence and then reflect on the alchemists whom we met. They all have different talents, often more than one. Many are not intellectually brilliant or even conventionally intelligent. Nor will intelligence in one area imply intelligence or talent in another. You can be linguistically gifted and speak five languages articulately but talk nonsense in all of them, be a brilliant pop musician but no good at maths, a skier of distinction but a lousy manager. This is obvious yet we still base our ideas of education on outdated and limited views of intelligence. We can end up classifying as stupid all those whose talents don't happen to fit what the examination systems require.

What is needed is an assumption by all concerned from the very beginning, that every small child has, in embryo, two or three different talents. These need to be identified and developed, even if they don't conform to the dictates of whatever core curriculum is in place at the time. After that, it has to be a matter of horses for courses or, in this case, fitting the courses to the horses. Some will want structures and rules throughout their lives, the better to express their talents, but those who show any sign of alchemy, be it through the traditional forms of creative processes or through endless curiosity and experiment, need to be given the space to express themselves. Naughty children may be the alchemists of the future and should not be stamped on too heavily. We have to wonder what would have happened had Richard Branson been conventionally clever at school. Would he have become just another brainy executive? Or if Dennis Stevenson had got his predicted brilliant degree and turned Cambridge academic?

Because talents are not always apparent at an early age people need to be exposed to an ever wider range of experiences as they grow up. Individuals, as we have seen, can stumble upon alchemy. As we have also noted, it is the process of schooling that is remembered more than the content – the teachers one met rather than the things they taught. There is much to be said, therefore, for expanding the process side of the curriculum even at the cost of losing some content. We could, for instance, end the classroom teaching part of the school day at lunchtime and use the afternoon for a large variety of activities, ranging from sport, music and drama to work experience, community projects, visits and projects of all sorts. The afternoons could be organized and run by an ancillary faculty drawn from the community.

In this way the young person would be exposed to a wider spectrum of adults, not all of them necessarily in the judgemental position of parent or teacher. It expands the chance of meeting a significant figure or mentor who can set one alight. It also provides more opportunities to discover what one is good at. The big Japanese corporations use a technique that can best be described as horizontal fast-tracking to develop or 'form' their high-potential recruits. They rotate them through a variety of assignments in different sections of the company, under a number of bosses, both so that they can get a clearer view of each person's capability but also so that individuals have a better chance to discover their talents and meet likely mentors. Alchemists like Martin Leach fashioned their own fast track before they stumbled upon the match between their talents and opportunities. It is a method that could and should be used in the formation of all our youth.

We should also be less fixated about keeping the young in schools until they are eighteen, and less anxious to see them go straight on to university if they do stay on to that age. Nearly half of our sample left school early and were probably right to do so. If they need more knowledge they know that they can always go back to college or courses later on, or pick it up from books or even the Internet. Education is not confined to educational institutions. 'You can learn anything if you really want to,' said Ozwald Boateng who, as we have seen, went off to study business methods when he realized that good tailoring wasn't enough by itself.

The chance to test your capabilities and interests in the world outside before settling for more expensive time-consuming education is surely desirable, even at the cost of losing some academic momentum. We should, therefore, encourage more 'gap' years, more short apprenticeships, more travel and more adventure. There are, in fact, signs that this is happening as the system becomes more flexible in response to the growing market in education.

There are also those whom we might call the hibernating alchemists, who have waited until mid-life or later to start something from nothing, perhaps because of the needs of a growing family, or because they had not yet discovered their particular talents. It took Tim Waterstone nearly twenty years before he put his dreams of book marketing to the test. Philip Hughes, while always a painter, was in his fifties before doing it full time. The concept of the Third Age, a period of life stretching from the end of formal work until one's seventies or later, opens up a new space for a new life, unknown to previous generations who mostly died within a few short years of retirement. Alchemy is not just for the young. Michael Young is still creating institutions in his eighties. The so-called 'Learning Society' will become a reality when people discover that they can reinvent their lives at any age, often by re-entering education. As William Atkinson has said of himself, most of us are still pregnant with possibilities, if we want to be.

Are women different, we had the temerity to wonder, or is their formation different? Those in our sample seem very representative of Britain at the moment. Julia Middleton, Rose Fenton and Lucy Neal of LIFT, Sabrina Guinness and Jane Tewson apply dedication and management expertise to social concerns. We could have replicated their examples many times over. London is bristling with social alchemists who are women. The same is true of small businesses. Joanne McFarlane and Mapi Lucchesi are typical gutsy women who have chosen to start commercial ventures on their own rather than work in a conventional organization.

A 1998 survey by Barclays Bank found that women were responsible for thirty per cent of small business start-ups. That may be a big understatement because they were looking at registered businesses not the independent trader who is classified as self-employed. They would have caught Mapi Lucchesi in their survey but not Joanne McFarlane.

There are, however, fewer women in our business category probably because fewer of these small start-ups go on to become milestone companies. They remain small-niche enterprises, which do not hit the headlines although, cumulatively, they make a big contribution to the community. Why should this be so? If we had searched outside London we could have sought to include women such as Anita Roddick of the Body Shop, Steve Shirley of FI or Delia Smith. Looking backwards there were past alchemists like Mary Quant in the Sixties, Prue Leith of restaurant fame or Sophie Merman of Sock Shop who were all alchemists in their time. We could also have thought of Vivienne Westwood the designer, or the River Café duo, Ruth Rogers and Rose Gray, who are well known in their fields. There are few today, however, who, starting from nothing, have built major industries and are London based and still in business.

Is it, maybe, something to do with the formation of women? All women now grow up expecting to work and have a career as well as, perhaps, a family. Do they inherit or acquire the assumption that to do both things well is difficult and that the commitment to full-time alchemy would exclude a husband and children? If so, our sample of women with families, sometimes large ones, would prove that assumption wrong, although no one should think that it is easy. Do women, during their formation, gain the impression that social activism is more respectable for them than business? If so, the vibrant examples of Joanne MacFarlane and Mapi Lucchesi, as well as Dee Dawson with her successful health business, should change their minds. Perhaps the incidental fact that 'entrepreneur' is a male term has subconscious ripples, which is one reason why we have preferred the neutral English word of 'alchemist'.

Another possibility is that the explanation lies in the formation of men, which accustoms them to the idea of women in a subsidiary role. If so, this tradition is surely out of date, although it may take a generation to make its way through to the workplace. Alchemy, however, needs approval from no one, only ambition and perseverance. Given those, as well as the femininity which is, we have suggested, part of the creative personality, there is no limit to what women alchemists can achieve. We sense that were we to be writing this book in twenty years' time there would be a much higher proportion of female business alchemists.

3 *In Summary*   Alchemy, we are now convinced, has its roots in the clusters of cities, and their immediate surrounds. It starts as a tender shoot, needing the comfort of like-minded folk and the support of necessary affiliates. Some imagine that the Internet will make cities unnecessary, that the whole world will be the alchemist's cluster. The Internet will make much possible and easy that was difficult before but just as virtual conferences are not as good as the real thing, virtual cities will never be the same as actual ones. A country, therefore, that wants to be creative, competitive and cultivated must reinvent its cities with particular emphasis on higher education and the arts.

Alchemists, we now believe, thrive on exposure to new situations. They get bored easily. They look for opportunities to make a difference and grab their luck. They want to be noticed and to express themselves in their work. So we should not shelter or protect our young so much or direct their formation too precisely before we or they know who they are. Too many are categorized by their early education and know no way to change categories. As careers become truncated, often ending in one's fifties, people need to be encouraged to rethink their lives for the twenty or thirty remaining active years.

Many of these ideas cannot be legislated into existence. They result more from fashion than from policy. We have created this book because, whatever we do to improve our cities or our systems of formation, we need as many models as are around of those who have gone before us to show what is possible when a woman or a man dares to dream of what might be and then decides to do it.

The New Alchemists

William Atkinson

(Phoenix School)

IN MARCH 1995 WILLIAM ATKINSON WAS asked by Christine Watford, the Director of Education at Hammersmith in west London, to write a report for her on Hammersmith School, an eleven–sixteen school which had just been failed by Ofsted, the schools inspectorate. He was, at the time, the Head of Cranford Community School and known as a successful head teacher. 'I have been into many bad schools' he told us, 'in Harlem and the Bronx, for instance, where they check the kids for guns when they arrive. But, apart from the guns, I had never been in such an awful school as the one I entered that day in Hammersmith. I was appalled – and angry. Appalled by the state of the place, the graffiti, the broken windows, the sense of chaos; and angry that those kids were being given such a rotten start in life.'

Those who write reports are often asked to implement them and so it was on this occasion. It took some persuading, but in April 1995 William Atkinson became Head of the Phoenix School. The change of name was one of his conditions, along with resources to clean up the physical appearance of the place, replace some furniture, buy textbooks and an agreement on more 'management space' to do what needed to be done. If anyone was able to turn what was by then base metal into the equivalent of gold – the old alchemists' dream – it had to be this man with his passion, conviction and forthright management style.

Four years later, William stands proudly in his gleaming school hall, underneath a banner with the emblems of some of the more than fifty different nationalities that gather there every day. The parents he is talking to have only one worry – that this man might leave. It is clear from his attitude that it is the young people who are the focus of his work. It is their lives that he wants to transform. The new uniforms he introduced, combined with the sense of decency and discipline, give the place an air of orderliness which, by all accounts, is totally new. The entry classes are full instead of half empty, now that the school is once again one of choice rather than that of last resort.

Has he succeeded in turning the place around? 'It is a long journey. It will never end, because one can never be satisfied. But we have made a start. The examination results are better, although still very poor, but then seventy-five per cent of our entry class are in the bottom twenty-two per cent of the national standards when they come here. Many can't speak English when they arrive but have to take examinations in English within six months and for almost all of them, anyway, it is not their native language. But the graffiti have gone, behaviour is much better. Ninety-five per cent of lessons are now judged to be satisfactory by Local Education Authority inspectors and some outstanding. Most of all we have, I think, changed expectations, the teachers' expectations of what the children can do and the childrens' expectations of themselves.'

William, rightly, is never going to be satisfied, but the visitor can clearly perceive a sense of purpose and of hope. The children, as William points out, come with some advantages mixed with their disadvantages. They may be bad at English but many of them speak four other languages because of their previous lives. A large number came to Britain as refugees and have learnt how to survive in adversity. The mix of nationalities can only be enriching, as the flags on display from an earlier gala performance demonstrate.

William is able to draw on his own experience. He was himself an immigrant, coming from Jamaica in 1957. Because his mother's English wasn't clear the ages of his elder brother and himself were confused when the two first went to school. The school thought that William, then seven, was nine and put him into the remedial class as being far behind for his age, while his nine-year-old brother, was put with the seven-year-olds. As a result, William has the unusual distinction of having failed the Eleven Plus examination *twice,* because he took it again when his real age was discovered. He then failed all GCSEs except history but, in a striking act of self-determination, decided to drop down a year and resit the exams. Why? Because he saw his brother, two years ahead of him, fail to get a job and realized that if he didn't pull himself together he would be condemned to a life of casual labour at the bottom of the heap.

Finally making the sixth form, he had the good fortune to meet an exceptional man, Ray Sanders, who was Sixth Form Head. 'This man took me seriously. He talked to me about my potential, about life as a journey. He started me believing in myself.' There were to be others later on, for example a Mr Woods in his first proper job, but Sanders set him on the path to his later achievements. Partly as a result of this experience, partly because he liked what he saw of the younger staff, he decided to be a teacher himself and was accepted by the Portsmouth College of Education. He still wasn't sure, so he took a 'gap' year to reflect, not on some spiritual trek to the Himalayas but as a drayman driving a beer lorry. It gave him time to read and think: 'I realized that I wanted to be with people, especially young people – so teaching it had to be.'

Teaching, however, was not going to be enough by itself. 'I wanted to capture an institution and so I started applying for deputy head jobs.' He tried and was rejected fifty times. William was undaunted: 'I promised myself that I would learn from every experience, including failure.' But the deputy job came eventually, followed by a succession of headships and a growing reputation as someone who could make a difference to a school, a person who was passionate about what he wanted, direct and tough-minded. He now sits on government task forces, is sought after for international conferences and visits, and is widely recognized as someone worth listening to.

Married, with four children, he laments the fact that his busy career meant that he saw less than he would have liked of his two eldest children when they were tiny. Maybe that is an unconscious repeat of his own childhood when his father was seldom even in the country and returned to Jamaica before William was nine, while his mother was up at five o'clock every morning to go to work in a factory, coming home exhausted at eight in the evening. 'Family support? Forget it!' He laughs. Unlike their father, however, William's children have his 'incredible' wife to organize their lives and support them. Does that make a difference? 'Definitely. I don't know how she does it, working in an autistic school four days a week but still being there for all of us.'

You have to wonder: if life had been easier for William at the beginning would he have found his resolve to take charge of it? Or if he had not met Roy Sanders at that crucial stage would he have gone on to 'capture an institution'? What seems clear is that he is doing everything he can to make sure that other young people's futures are not left to such chance events.

And the future? 'I'm still pregnant. I want to make a difference wherever I can.'

Robert Ayling

(British Airways' New Head Office)

ROBERT AYLING IS CHIEF EXECUTIVE OF British Airways. He did not, of course, create that respected and long-established airline. He is featured in this book of alchemists, however, because of what he was responsible for creating, a most unusual and original place of work at the very heart of the company.

Not many chief executives are granted the chance to bring into being a physical expression of their beliefs about people and organizations. Such an opportunity came to Robert Ayling soon after his arrival at British Airways as Company Secretary in 1985. At a Board meeting that year Gordon Dunlop, the company's Finance Director, put forward a proposal to buy a plot of land beside the A4 just west of Heathrow Airport. It was the local rubbish dump in part of the green belt, which Gordon thought might be a possible site for new offices if planning permission were ever to be granted in such a protected area.

Twelve years later, on 19 December 1997, Ayling, now Chief Executive, moved with the builders and the first 200 staff into what is now Waterside, the head-offices of British Airways. It is a striking building. Rather, it is six separate ones which back on to a central street but face out to parkland and gardens. Each section is slightly different, with its own character, but all are built around courtyards. In them are no individual offices or desks but small open-plan group areas. The street is a real street with a café, a bank and a branch of Waitrose where you can place your order via computer and pick it up in the car-park on the way home. There are trees, a piazza and a small stream, all under a high glass canopy.

Robert is pictured in the piazza, where he can also be seen having coffee with his wife Julia, an important influence in his life and, on the steps, meeting with a member of staff. Organizations, he says, work best if they are designed as villages. 'In a village you don't learn what is going on by reading memos, you go down the street and pick up the news by bumping into people.' Randomness, he believes, and accidental meeting, encourages serendipity, removes the impression of hierarchy and fosters a sense of comradeship and belonging. The building is a delight to the eye. Those who work there confirm that it lifts the heart just to enter it. Many say that it would be hard to work anywhere else. It is a sort of modern-day cathedral, albeit one dedicated to a corporate enterprise.

Robert is sure that the building has changed the culture of the head office and, eventually, he hopes, of the airline. He can't, he says, lose his temper or rather, when he does, very, very occasionally, everyone knows immediately because it is a place of no secrets. Meetings take place more casually, in the café or on the steps. Communication is hugely improved because people bump into each other in the street rather than in the lavatories – the usual place for informal conversations in such institutions. There are, deliberately, no lifts from the underground car-parks so that everyone has to pass through the street on the way to their work place, meeting people on the way. First names are the norm and no one stands on ceremony – you can't in a village street.

It is all very different from the old offices at Speedbird House which was 'a genuinely horrible building'. Depressing long corridors were lined with boxes for individual offices. Long, solitary days were punctuated only by the arrival of the tea lady. People met only by appointment so that diaries were completely filled with internal meetings. Your place in the hierarchy was evident from the size and décor of your individual box. It was a dingy, compartmentalized world, which inevitably coloured the atmosphere or culture of the whole organization.

It was one which Ayling was determined to change when he became Managing Director and later Chief Executive. Gordon Dunlop's imaginative purchase gave him the opportunity. It had taken four years of public hearings to get permission to turn the rubbish dump into a park for the local community with a spectacular office in the middle of it. A visionary architect was found in Niels Torp who had built the head offices of SAS in Sweden, also designed around the idea of a street. Ayling is the first to point out that there were many others involved, particularly Gwilym Rees-Jones and Chris Byron who, at different times, led the project team. They had, as it happened, both been cabin crew managers in their time and were very much 'people' people, but it was Ayling who lent his passion to the project and made sure that it would embody his own beliefs and values.

How had this man who started life in his father's grocer's shop and later became a lawyer, then a civil servant, acquired the understanding of the crucial relationship between space and behaviour? 'I had a very good education,' he says, 'but it had no visual component.' Luckily, aged twenty-five, he met Julia Crallan, an artist and the daughter of an architect. She took him to Venice and 'gave me a three-day lecture' on buildings and the visual arts. They married and her influence on his thinking is quite clear, but he also got to know and admire her father, from whom he learnt about buildings and the 'manipulation of space'. This to him was the definition of architecture. But a lawyer? He looked surprised at the question. 'A lawyer's work is all about people' he insisted. 'All our case law deals with the stories of individuals. That's why it is so satisfying.'

His own experience convinced him of the importance of physical space. His lawyer's office was light and airy with huge picture windows. The civil service was very different in atmosphere and physical space, only eclipsed by the ghastly experience of Speedbird House. He knew, by then, that behaviour would change in improved surroundings. He was, he admits, lucky to have been given the chance, lucky in the chosen architect, but visionary architects need visionary clients to make the most of situations. Niels Torp and Robert Ayling together have created something special in the way of work places and in so doing have made a huge difference to the lives of the now 3000 people who work or visit there. The training centre is deliberately placed in the middle of the structure so that all those who come in for training, as everyone does at some point, get the message of the building.

Anyone who has visited or worked in the old Speedbird House and has been to Waterside would be happy to confirm that Ayling and his colleagues have performed a stunning piece of alchemy. As the information revolution begins to affect the nature and organization of work as fundamentally as the industrial revolution did, there will be more pressures to redesign the actual physical surroundings. Robert Ayling's example should spur all those with any responsibility to take the opportunity to make as much of a statement as he has and to express their beliefs in stone and steel and glass.

Trevor Baylis

(Inventor)

YOU DON'T NORMALLY ENTER A HOUSE via the indoor swimming pool, nor find the office in the bedroom, but then Trevor Baylis has never been conventional and he built this house himself to suit himself. The real point of the house, however, is something that even he could not manufacture – it is the situation, on a bend overlooking the Thames where, in his roof-top garden, he reads or watches the world of the river go by, with his dog and faithful companion, Monty, at his feet. When, that is, he isn't inventing things or, nowadays, inventing institutions.

He takes up a rather strange-looking object, winds a handle and out comes the sound of a cricket commentary. This is the clockwork radio he invented. He puts another one down on the deck in the sun and out comes Radio 1. It's his solar radio. Neither of them needs batteries or electricity. Nor does his wind-up torch. Yet to come are personally pow-ered two-way radios, mine detectors and water purification units. You can buy these things in the high street, but their real value is in Africa where electricity is rare and batteries are too expensive for all but the affluent. If AIDS is ever brought under control there it may well be in part thanks to Trevor Baylis whose radios are the only means of spread-ing information and health education to large tracts of that continent.

That's why he did it, in fact. He was watching a programme on AIDS in Africa which lamented the fact that there was no cheap way of accessing the mass of people with the facts about the disease. He went down to his workshop beside the swimming pool and within an hour had connected a spring to a small dynamo and got it working. A few more touches with the soldering iron and he had a wind-up radio. Twenty-five seconds of winding now gives you an hour's listening. For Trevor that was the easy bit. 'Invention is just problem-solving,' he says. 'We can all do it if we want to. I bet a thousand chaps slapped them-selves on the forehead and said "Why didn't I think of that?"' The next bit was more difficult.

No one was interested in his radio – the lament of too many British alchemists down the centuries. The next twelve months were dreadful. He still has a framed letter from the Design Council, saying it was a nice idea that just wasn't practicable. Others said that it couldn't work with-out a spring weighing a hundredweight, even though he was standing there with the thing in his hand. Trevor was lucky. The BBC programme *Tomorrow's World* featured the invention. An unusual accountant, Christopher Staines of Stoy Hayward, saw it and said that his firm could make it happen. The BBC World Service liked it too. A South African businessman, driving in his car, heard Trevor talking about it on the radio, came immediately to London and wrote out a cheque for £750,000. Lynda Chalker of the Overseas Development Agency ('bless her!') put up another £150,000. They were in business.

Bay Gen in Cape Town now manufactures 60,000 of the radios a month, in a factory worked by disabled people. Trevor has some shares in the business and a small royalty: 'I'm asset rich but income poor.' But money for Trevor, sixty-one years old and with no family, has never been the point of life, although it's nice to have no cash flow problems for once. He may yet turn out to have helped to change Africa but that has never been his ambition in life either: 'I'm not carrying the cross of Jesus, I'm carrying a soldering iron.' He had used his soldering iron to good effect before, inventing a range of little gadgets which he called Orange Aids to help disabled people manage their everyday lives more easily. That business was taken away from him by the bank: 'I was systematically done over.' But even if he realized no money for himself, he made life easier for a great number of people.

His ambition now is to make sure that other inventors don't have to suffer the rejections and discouragements that he endured in order to bring their products to market. He is determined to create an academy of inventors, perhaps located in the old Patents Office. The academy would counsel potential inventors and, if their products looked viable, would work with them to set up a business. Inventing institutions is more tedious than inventing radios but Trevor is determined and, in alchemy, determination is half the battle.

As a result of his radio he has been awarded the OBE, starred in *This Is Your Life* and a BT television ad, been made a professor and collected four files of clippings – 'my ego files'. He's tickled pink at this late recognition of his talents but, in fact, water, not inventions, has occupied most of his life. He swam for Britain and the army in his youth and earned his living, once he left after National Service, by selling swimming pools, doing stunt swimming and teaching the sport to schoolchildren. 'I was employed as an engineer by a swimming pool company but early on, at the pre-opening day of the Ideal Home Exhibition, I asked my boss if I could try out the pool. I dived in and swam around for a bit, looked up and saw a crowd watching me. "Don't stop" my boss said. "We're selling pools!"' That became his life for many years, stunt and comedy swimming to sell pools.

Fortunately for us, the lathe and the soldering iron had always been a part of his life since he worked beside his father in his toolshed at home. His family, in Kilburn, was 'decent but poor' but 'poverty is a great leveller' and Trevor, the only child, had a happy childhood except for one horrifying experience. He was raped by the curate at his local Sunday school when he was five. He says that he has never again been able to trust people, something which, he believes, has accounted for many of his difficulties in business.

A psychiatrist he consulted also theorized that it may even be the reason for his irresistible desire to show off, in order to compensate for the feelings of inadequacy and insecurity which the incident provoked. Certainly, gregarious and an extrovert, he never lacked for friends. Then he failed his Eleven Plus exam. It was a blessing in disguise because the secondary modern school where he went had workshops. When he left, at fifteen, he studied for a Higher National Certificate in the evenings and ended up with a working knowledge of every sort of engineering – mechanical, electrical, structural and soil. His workshop now shares the honours with the swimming pool in his house.

You feel, with Trevor Baylis, that he has his world sorted out with a stock of ideas yet to come, to be turned into useful products. What is his secret? The swimming stunts, alarming to observers, that he has done all his life have helped to build up his self-confidence, although it's hard to believe that it was ever lacking: 'you've got to have an ego, although too much of it makes you unpopular.' He still likes to have that ego massaged and who can blame him. The roar of the crowds can be a great boost to morale.

His father's example and encouragement helped early on, he says. Later, two swimming coaches and his colleagues let him know they believed he had talent. Then there are his ideas about life. He believes fervently that convention is an obstacle to progress, and that it is part of human nature to explore and to question. Given those convictions and his experience that the simplest solutions are best, it is easy to see how Trevor Baylis ends up as a perpetual alchemist, infectious in his enthusiasm for the possibilities that lie ahead but always at heart remaining a rebel.

Ozwald Boateng
(Tailor)

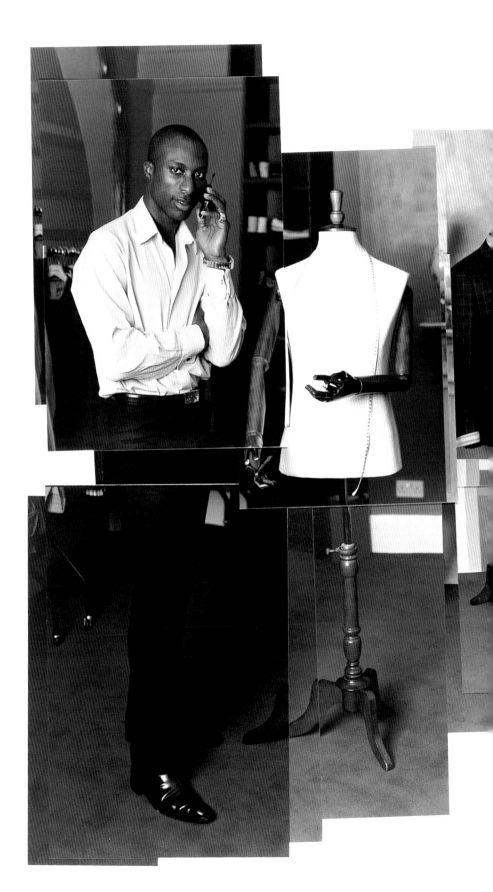

OZWALD BOATENG HAS BEEN CALLED THE 'Peacock of Savile Row' and his sensuous materials, glowing colours and sculptured suits sit as oddly and as picturesquely in that traditional world as a peacock on the lawn of a country estate. Why did he go there with his revolutionary approach to the design of what men wear and how they might look? Because it was traditionally the place for the best and Ozwald wanted to prove that he deserved to be there. Because he wanted to do more than run a tailoring business; he wanted to change attitudes. Did they accept him in the Street? Yes, he says, after a time, because they respect what he does and because he has brought in new life and new cus-tomers and they have seen their activities increase overall by twenty per cent.

That habit of creating challenges for himself has been the story of Ozwald's short life. He is thirty years old but he is already on his third company. Along the way he founded the first couture house for men, held the first catwalk show for men's fashions in Paris, has dressed many of the famous in the worlds of the media, rock music and politics, been featured in newspapers and journals around the world, made ten short films, presented shows on both radio and television, and appeared on *Question Time* on TV. He has also gone bankrupt, been divorced and fallen out with his first business partner.

Those three débâcles all happened in the spring of 1998. His busi-ness, both the ready-made and the made-to-measure parts of it, was turning over £3 million a year when orders from Hong Kong and Japan worth nearly £2 million were unexpectedly cancelled as the Far East downturn took hold. He was already in the midst of splitting with his business partner and parting from his wife when the receivers walked in. He owed £50,000 to the bank and had nothing to pay them with. It was not the happiest moment of his life.

A week later came the day of reckoning. The receivers wanted to sell the business, but it was, as they knew, worth nothing without Ozwald so they offered him the chance to buy it back. After some haggling a price was agreed. Then they turned to him and said, 'Right, let's get this over with Boateng, get out your cheque-book.'

'I haven't got any money,' he replied. 'Can you lend it to me?'

They looked at him in astonishment. 'You've got to be joking,' they said.

So he made them another offer 'Give me time to pay.' They did, and within a week he was up and running again, helped by a lot of publicity, which had started off gloating at his downfall but ended up respecting his phoenix-like recovery. Six months later his turnover was back to £1.2 million a year and his staff of sixteen were overworked.

Alchemists have the extraordinary ability to turn disaster into new life but it is always what is euphemistically called 'a learning experience'. In other words it hurts. BOATENG GOES BUST was all over the papers. It wasn't the sort of publicity he was used to, but 'I look at problems a lot differently now. I now say, "That didn't work, well let's try this." I was very entrepreneurial as a boy,' he adds, 'I hired out pirated videos at school when I was thirteen, and I wanted to buy a house and rent it out at fourteen but my mother wouldn't lend me the money. The house doubled in value in a year.'

He left school at sixteen to study computers, but fell in love while he was doing it. 'She was incredibly artistic and believed that you could do anything you wanted to. She was doing a college fashion show and asked me to help. I said "I can't make clothes" but she showed me and I was amazed to find how easy it was.' They broke up after two years but he enrolled for a diploma in fashion design: 'I wanted to show her.'

In fact, he already had a small company going because he found that his friends liked and bought his clothes, and while at college he had sold his first collection to a big London store. How did he learn the technical bits of tailoring? 'Once you decide on something you can always learn it. I took garments apart to see how they were made and experimented – what would happen if . . .? And I found out who the best tailors were and hassled them to find out how they did it. I was young and eager and they didn't mind too much.' From eighteen to twenty-one he sold his suits mainly to a large London store. They all sold out but not much money came in.

So Ozwald did a six-month crash course in business. 'I could do a fantastic business plan but I needed £1.5 million to start it. I travelled the world but no one would back it. I decided "better get back to reality again but maybe I will try it in New York".' But his new love, a top model, persuaded him to stay in London and marry her. 'Women have always changed my life!'

He set up his business at home. Then came the really big gamble. He put all the money he had, and some of his wife's, into a catwalk show in Paris. 'You're mad' everyone said. 'No one has ever done a male catwalk show. No one knows you in Paris. No one will come.' He ignored them all, worked his heart out talking to anyone he could find about his ideas and the gamble paid off. Astonished by his brashness, perhaps, the world came to his show. He got huge media coverage describing his 'new concept of tailoring'. He was off and running, to Savile Row and Wimpole Street. Alchemy needs bravado.

Ozwald Boateng is the third child of Ghanaian parents who left Ghana before he was born to live in Crouch End. They are both from the Ashanti people and Ozwald speaks proudly of their long lineage. He has always had, therefore, something to live up to. But, importantly, at the age of five his father told him, almost as a prophecy, 'You are going to be successful.' 'So I had that responsibility from a very young age. Everyone was waiting.' And the tailoring? 'I only thought about it recently but my mother was always sewing with her Singer machine. I wore my first proper suit at five, handmade by her. And she taught me about money. She used to trust me to buy some things for the house and she would give me the rent to pay. My brother, too, was my great champion and still is. I get great support from my family.'

What comes next, one wonders for this talented, exciting, rather dashing man? In the short term he is going to be more designer than tailor and needs urgently to delegate the day-to-day management of his business so that he has more time for creativity – and for a family one day perhaps. 'Work, work, work' was a major contributor to the break-up of his last marriage, he acknowledges ruefully. In the longer term, he has offers of all sorts spilling through his letter-box – TV and film roles particularly. Ozwald can't imagine an end to the urge to make a difference or, as he puts it 'to take the traditional and change it. I have learnt never to say never. I want to find out what else I can do. We will all do lots of different things in the new world that is coming.'

Richard Branson

(Virgin)

A RECENT BRITISH TABLOID POLL FOUND that its readers ranked Richard Branson as the most intelligent man in Britain. That wasn't the way his teachers thought of him back in his schooldays. He was, by his own account, 'pretty hopeless' in the classroom. He was, in fact, dyslexic – a word unknown in those days – and he still is. 'I look at a crossword puzzle and I just go blank . . . We are Britain's largest private company and I still can't work out the difference between gross and net.'

Could that be true of the man who has built a commercial empire with an estimated annual revenue of over £2 billion with some forty principal companies, almost all started from scratch, whose airline is one of the more profitable in the business and whose venture into the financial services business has transformed that sector? Maybe it is true, because money, he insists, although 'necessary to pay the bills' and useful for his start-ups, has never been the point of any of his ventures. 'My businesses grow out of my experiences, usually my bad experiences. I see something done badly which I know that we could do better – like the airline. No one was offering their customers a decent service. I was sure that whoever did so would not only have a successful company but would also change the whole industry.' Virgin Atlantic proved his point. 'Everyone told me that the quickest way to bankruptcy was to make a million and then start an airline' but he knew he could do it his way.

'I turn my fascinations into businesses,' he also says. First was a ground-breaking student magazine, which led to the Student Advisory Centre, sparked by his girlfriend's difficulty in getting an abortion back in the Sixties. Then came Virgin Records and his first commercial success with the signing of Mike Oldfield and his *Tubular Bells* album. Then came the airline and, growing older, the financial services venture, Virgin Direct. Now he's considering entering the mobile phone market because a friend was convinced that his brain tumour was caused by mobile phones. So Branson wants to market safe ones. As he grows older there are plans for a game reserve in Africa and the creation of the most beautiful hotel in the world. 'There is always a market for the best,' he maintains and then, 'the bottom line sorts itself out.'

He is the most public of businessmen. In a recent survey ninety-six per cent of the respondents had heard of Virgin and ninety-five per cent knew that it was Branson's company. Nowadays he energetically promotes himself in order to publicize his brand, donning a wedding gown to launch his bridal fashions venture and driving a tank through Times Square to promote his Virgin Cola. Yet he is also a home-loving family man. He chose to be photographed for this book in the kitchen of his family house in the country, which seems to be the heart of his life, and he resolutely keeps the school holidays free for his two children and his wife Joan. His business ventures follow him everywhere, however. In his kitchen he is as likely to be on the phone or talking to one of his staff as cooking a meal. On holiday with the family he gets up at dawn to do his business stuff before they are awake. He can't, it seems, stop starting things.

So how did this paradoxical man get to be what he is at the age of forty-eight? Could it be that the misfortune of dyslexia was the unintended cause of his later fortunes? Maybe, he agrees. 'I had to rebel at school because I wasn't excelling in class.' At first he turned to athletics for that bit of excellence – and at eleven was triumphant, winning all the cups and prizes. But then he ruined his cartilage in a tackle on the football field, which meant the end of competitive sports. Blocked on the sports field he turned to commerce and a career of serial alchemy.

He was also fortunate in his parents. The eldest of three children, he was encouraged from an early age to be self-reliant and adventurous. The most attractive part of his autobiography is the account of his boyhood and his obvious admiration for his parents. They tolerated his early schoolboy ventures into business – a Christmas tree plantation in the field behind the house (eaten by rabbits in the first months) and a budgie-breeding scheme (no market), and allowed him to leave school early to start his student magazine 'although we did walk around the garden a few times.'

He was only sixteen and, for someone who was dyslexic and number blind, a magazine was a brave, even foolhardy, undertaking. Like most first ventures it required total involvement, no cash and lots of dedication but, insists Branson, it was fun, as he believes all work should be. It never made money but it launched him as a public figure, particularly after his Student Advisory Centre prosecuted a policeman for planting drugs on one of their clients. In retaliation Richard was arrested on an old nineteenth-century law forbidding the mention of venereal disease in public advertisements. He was found guilty and fined a token £7 but by then his face and his cause were well known.

Criticized by some for his impulsiveness, even for his courting of the crowd, Richard Branson is admired by the general public who are in favour of the simplicity of his approach and his David against Goliath stance in taking on traditional interests. They like his approach to business and don't begrudge him his riches, which they see as earned by his own efforts. Rather ingenuously, he says that he and his colleagues didn't even realize that they had a brand until a few years ago, although he now knows that it is their most important asset and does everything he can to promote it. 'I joke now that I ought to be known as Brand-son' he says.

The simplicity of his approach carries over to his managerial style, which some have criticized for being too casual. He maintains, however, that if you have the right people in place, treat them well and trust them, they will produce happy customers and the necessary profits to carry on and expand the work. Part of him is still a young boy at heart, which contributes to his charm, with a boyish love of adventure, challenges and sense of fun, as exemplified in his series of balloon flights, which everyone recognized were highly dangerous but, he says, were worth doing for the excitement they aroused among young children everywhere. Less dangerously, the forty-eight-year-old Branson was recently to be seen dressed up as a can of Virgin Cola in Shinjuku Station Square, promoting his brand but having fun.

He has had his occasional failures or difficulties, although he would call them learning experiences, referring particularly to his brushes with the financiers in the City. There is also the Virgin Rail Group, a different sort of challenge, which some think he should not have taken on because this was not a new business started from scratch, but an old business, with old rolling stock, that had to be turned round. Richard is undaunted by the criticism his railway has attracted. 'I will take a bet that in three years' time people will be saying it is by far the best railway, with new trains and more trains, faster times and dedicated staff.' Once again, he saw something done badly which he believed that he could do much better. In the meantime, however, he has to bear the damage which the business he has acquired may do to his brand. That is what makes it the most challenging of all his ventures so far.

Richard Branson is not going to stop or rest. He loves what he does and it shows. Some worry that he may stretch the brand too far, or that managing his infinite variety of enterprises will overstretch even his capacity for the personal relationships, which seem to be crucial to his style, but this is a man excited by life and all its possibilities, who has never taken 'no' for an answer and for whom the world is a bundle of possibilities waiting to be explored. He may get it wrong occasionally but that won't deter him or detain him. Few have started so many businesses or provided good fun jobs for so many – 25,000 at the last count.

Terence Conran
(Design/Restaurants)

THE UNMISTAKABLE CONRAN STYLE OF THE room, the love of good cooking, the cigar, the smile of a man who is living life to the full at sixty-seven and obviously revelling in it – this is Sir Terence Conran at home in his London penthouse apartment above his office at Butlers Wharf near Tower Bridge.

This man has been affecting our living in, and our eating out for four decades, and he is still at it. With Habitat, he changed the way we furnished our homes back in the Sixties. In the Nineties his restaurants, eleven in London alone at the last count, have helped to set a new trend in eating out. Some say, perhaps even enviously hope, that he has lost his touch, but instead his plans get more outrageous as he gets older – a refurbished Great Eastern Hotel with six restaurants opening before the end of the century and a massive diner and Conran shop in the derelict space under a bridge in the middle of Manhattan, what he calls 'a cathedral', something which will, he believes, reinvigorate a whole area of that city.

But no, he says, he isn't trying to change the world, just doing all the things he has a passion for, surrounded by people he enjoys working with, most of them young. 'I'm in the excitement business.' And, because it is his own, he can make his enthusiasms happen without having to ask permission from anyone else, such as shareholders who tend to be impatient for early rewards. Is it about money, then? Well, he obviously has pots of the stuff and his group is predicting a turnover of £150 million in 2000, double the performance of 1997, but money seems to be more the score-card than the point, as well as the means of funding some new enthusiasm.

By following his gut instincts he believes that he will be proved right in the end. Not that he always has – his industrial magnate days as chief of Storehouse, the retail group, ended in his departure. Butlers Wharf was a dream of a development that ran into trouble in the recession and had to be sold. Failure, however, he regards as a necessary part of pioneering and Conran is nothing if not a pioneer with, you sense, a low boredom threshold. 'We look at the print out of the sales of all our enterprises every Monday,' he says, 'but I am really at the design end of the business, leaving others to manage the operations'. Not content with designing his projects, he can't keep his hands off the real thing. He has a furniture factory employing thirty-five people in the old farmyard of his country home.

Conran's mother had creativity in her bloodstream but married into a world and a time where women were not expected to have careers. Instead, she applied it to the education of Terence and his sister, for which he is everlastingly grateful. One of his earliest memories is of finding, as a tiny child, a pot of green paint at the bottom of the kitchen cupboard and spilling it all over the terracotta floor. 'I remember thinking then that it was a horrible mix of colours!' His mother encouraged him to make things for her, set up a workshop for him and a pottery kiln in the garden. Aged twelve and convalescing from a burst appendix, he made dolls' house furniture which sold in the local shop.

His mother's insistence on a creative education took him to Bryanston during the war years where he met some of the country's leading craftspeople who, having been classified as conscientious objectors, were then teaching. Wars have unexpected dividends. 'They were extraordinary people. Don Potter taught me sculpture and metalwork. Charles Handley Read, who put together a great collection of Victorian furniture, was a fantastic teacher with an enormous knowledge of the arts.' But Terence wasn't brilliant academically so he left at sixteen with, of all things, an ambition to be a gunsmith. 'I was fascinated by the craftsmanship and the aesthetic beauty. But then I found out that it involved a ten-year apprenticeship!' So it was off to study Textile Design at the Central School of Art and Design, to Dora Batty the visionary head and Eduardo Paolozzi, the sculptor, one of the visiting faculty who was to be a big influence in more ways than one – 'he introduced me to risotto nero!'

Terence does not seem to have had much patience with schools and courses. He left Central after a year to work with an architect designing furniture and textiles, including major commissions for the Festival of Britain. That finished and aged twenty, 'unemployed and unemployable' he started making furniture in the basement of Ballet Rambert, his first commission being the furniture for the office of the *Architectural Review*. Still short of cash, he and a friend pondered how they might make money. 'A place where people like us could eat cheaply' seemed a possibility. Terence went to Paris to work as a '*plongeur*' to find out how things worked behind the scenes. He came back convinced that chefs were authoritarian brutes. 'We needed a restaurant without cooks!' The answer was a soup kitchen in London's Chandos Place, fitted out with his own furniture, which sold soup and a chunk of French bread for 1/6d. 'But the real draw was the second Espresso machine in London.' Food and furniture, the unusual combination that was to be the pattern of much of his life, was established here.

Habitat came next – out of frustration. The retailers weren't displaying his furniture the proper way, so he was obliged to start his own shop. He eventually had to take Habitat public in order that the shares he had given to his work-force could be assessed at a marketable value. Then Terence started collecting other people's shops and chains – Mothercare, Richards, Heals, FNAC, Blazer, British Home Stores – and entered his phase as the head of a public company with Storehouse. The idea was that his design flair could be applied to revive these ailing brands and in cases like Mothercare it worked very successfully.

But Terence Conran was a creator more than he was a manager and, after installing a chief executive and a chairman to replace his dual role in Storehouse, he retreated to the world he was more familiar with. 'I said to myself, "Cut your losses, kid, go and do the things you would like to do yourself."' This turned out to be the ambitious idea of turning Butlers Wharf into a stunning mixed development of the arts, business, residences and eateries. Luck, for once, was not on his side. The recession of the Eighties forced him out and he still grieves over what might have been, as he looks out on the crammed blocks of flats and offices going up all around him in what is now a highly successful development.

Terence Conran is unusual in that his life has not deviated much from how it started out with that first dolls' house. A mix of creative design and business flair, a persistent interest in the way that people live and a desire to make it better, a perpetual itch to create and to work with exciting people, preferably young – his instincts and dreams have simply grown with the years and with his ambitions.

You get the feeling, talking to him now, that the best of his work is yet to come, that all his working life has been a preparation for the grandiose projects which are currently in progress or are still to be conceived. First it was London, then Paris and Tokyo, then New York – next the world? What is his secret? He says it is simple – style and quality, both of which will always find a market and need the right people. 'It's terribly important to me that I like my colleagues. We run a mutual appreciation society.'

Dee Dawson

(First Anorexic Clinic)

THE SUREST WAY TO UNLEASH Dr Dee Dawson's talents and energy is to tell her that something is impossible. 'Never take no for an answer' is part of her philosophy, as it is with most of the alchemists we have met.

She is pictured today with some of her staff and patients outside the anorexia clinic that she started in her home, Rhodes Farm, in Mill Hill eight years ago. It was the first and is still the only such clinic in Britain, with thirty-two beds. In those eight years she has changed the lives of several hundred young people and their families, and made herself a comfortable income into the bargain. Yet nine years earlier, on a family holiday in France, she went to meet her husband at the airport to find him sitting at the bar with his head in his hands. He had gone back to London for four days to see if all was well with his phenomenally successful computer company, only to find that his staff had literally run off with his business, wiped his files and codes, and transferred all the staff and clients to their own new venture down the road.

The Dawsons were broke. She was just finishing, at forty-two, her long seven-year training to be a doctor. The cars that belonged to his company and the lease of the building were financed by their personal guarantees, which had not, of course, been taken on by his ex-employees. They had four young children, all in private schools, and Dee was eight months pregnant with a fifth. Her husband was too shocked and depressed to do anything and his firm was irrecoverable. Their only assets were a nice house with a large garden and Dee's education – an MBA from the London Business School plus her medical qualification. She searched for some way to make use of these assets while still looking after children and husband. There was a need waiting to be filled, her training and experience told her. Surely parents and health authorities would pay for places at a residential treatment centre for anorexic children.

It had never been done. They told her it couldn't be done. That was enough for Dee. Dora Black, one of the leading child psychiatrists in the country, whom she had met during her medical training, agreed to be the consultant. With her name on board the medical insurance companies agreed to recognize the clinic. That done, Dee rang the Anorexia Association: 'I've opened a clinic today' she told them boldly. The

Association sent her her first patient. She then contacted the TV programme *London Tonight* and suggested that they might want to televise her new place. They were surprised to find only one patient but came along. Within six months she had six more patients, the house was full, her own family all had to sleep in one room, but the bills were getting paid.

It had been a fraught experience, but from then on it was a question of building on success. There are now two full-time child psychiatrists and a team of very competent nurses, cooks and teachers. Dee's role is today largely administrative. The house was extended some years back and the family moved out, to the dismay of her children who enjoyed the company of the other kids and who helped, in those first years, to create the sense of a loving family home which was so important to the success of Rhodes Farm. Dee is beginning to itch for another challenge.

Looking back, it is all part of a pattern, one that might stand as a model for budding alchemists. Born to working-class parents who took little interest in her education or, indeed, in her subsequent career, Dee always had to make her own running. At university she decided to abandon her course on the spur of the moment to follow her fiancé to Madagascar, having just waved him goodbye at Exeter station. 'Do it now' turns out to be another of her philosophies. Back in London, two years later, and married, her long-felt desire to be a doctor surfaced, so she went to university once more, to study biochemistry, only to be turned down twice by medical schools in spite of a good degree. Undaunted, she went to Newcastle to do a doctorate in biochemistry, having met the right professor by chance on a train. But a doctorate was not to be an instant passport to medical school. 'You're knocking at a door that will never be open to you as a woman,' the dean of the medical school said to her. 'Go away and do something different.'

She packed her bags that same afternoon, abandoning her doctorate, went to London and into a business career. For that, she reckoned, she needed an MBA. The London Business School turned her down. 'So I rang them up. I said "I need this, and I'm good, you can't do this to me." They relented and let me in because, they said, of my persistence.' Then followed a patch of business alchemy. A chance conversation at the bar with a potential backer led to her setting up Dee Dawson Outsize Fashions, an enterprise which flourished for a while, then languished.

Dee was bored – 'If we're not going to impress the world, why bother?' – and pregnant. 'What would you like to be doing?' her gynaecologist asked her. 'I want to do what you're doing' she said and remembered her desire to be a doctor. Now aged thirty-four it wasn't going to be easy. She was advised to take chemistry A levels again. She did, successfully, but still the Royal Free Hospital turned her down. She was used to this and phoned them up: 'You can't do this; I know you accepted someone aged thirty-five last year. Why not me? I'll be great.' She got in. After five years of courses and exams came the regulation 'house jobs'. She had four children by now. She couldn't possibly spend all her hours on duty. Why not a job share? No, she was told, it had never been done, it was impossible. That was enough. She and a colleague wrote to every consultant they could think of and, eventually, were jointly accepted for a house job at the North Middlesex Hospital – the first job share at that level in the NHS.

Dee was planning a career as a management consultant specializing in health care. After all there aren't that many consultants who are both doctors and MBAs. But then came that fateful holiday and the theft of her husband's business. The next years were hard work – alchemy always is – but she now has an established success on her hands. Was she passionate about anorexia? 'No, it was a market opportunity, but one worth doing. What I'm passionate about is setting up things that work.' Wasn't it risky? 'No, for me the set-up costs were low. We had the house and I came free. And at the time things couldn't get much worse.' She had been right in her analysis. There *was* a need for a dedicated residential centre for anorexics, and the health authorities and insurance companies *were* prepared to pay, once her credentials were established.

Alchemists are sensible about risk and passionate about making a difference in some way. And Dee's self-confidence, where did that come from? 'Well, my grandparents were shopkeepers, entrepreneurs in their own way, maybe I caught it from them. . . . And yes, I had one fantastic teacher, in biology. I got the best GCSE grade in biology for the whole board. He was very pleased by that. Then I knew that I wasn't stupid.'

'You build mountains for yourself to climb' her mother told her once reprovingly. Some would think that silly, as her sister does, for one.

'Don't make it sound easy' said Dee herself, 'because it isn't.' But for alchemists like Dee Dawson it is what makes life worth living.

Declan Donnellan and Nick Ormerod

(Theatre Director and Designer
– Cheek by Jowl)

DECLAN (ON THE RIGHT) AND NICK are pictured in their London garden. Carefully planted so as to look totally natural, it has echoes of Nick's designs for the theatre company, Cheek by Jowl, which they, together, created and run. They formed the company in 1981 and, since then, they have become truly international, taking their plays to over forty countries. In London all fifteen of Donnellan's and Ormerod's productions have been nominated for Olivier awards since the Most Promising Newcomer Award in 1985. Their work is highly respected both for its insight as well as for its entertainment value.

Many people start theatre companies and direct plays, but few last as long as Cheek by Jowl, are as successful or set a new standard and style of production. As designer and director these two people bring fresh insights to familiar classics. Working in a close partnership they do everything that they can, in both design and production, to get rid of anything that stands in the way of the shared experience by actors and audience. It is on their international tours, where often the actual words may not be understood by many in the audience, that their work has to be honed to its sparest elements.

They have promised a new and exhilarating style of theatre out of nothing but their imagination. Each play, indeed each performance, is a new creation. Declan has even been known to rehearse the cast one more time before the final night, in the firm belief that each performance has to express something fresh. You could say that their craft is one of continuous alchemy. They founded the enterprise and they own it, but it is truly a company (literally a group of companions) in which the work is far more important than the proceeds.

After seventeen years, however, they feel that they need a personal sabbatical. They have, therefore, closed the company down for a while in order to explore new areas and ideas in their work, turning their backs on their principal source of personal income. 'Work', says Declan 'is more important than a career.' He means that in order to give of your personal best you have to take control of your life, whatever the financial cost.

The official biographies of the two men are identical since 1981, after which their lives and their work intertwined. The portrait demonstrates this, showing them contemplating a new project together on their garden bench, sharing a drink (on the left) and setting off again into the world outside. They met at Cambridge University nine years earlier, both wanting to discover the world of theatre and art where they sensed they would get closer to the truth of things. Before that, however, they had known rather different worlds.

Nick, the second son of a doctor, had experienced a conventional privileged English upbringing of preparatory school and boys' public school, none of which he enjoyed. He had become a withdrawn young man as a result.

Declan's parents were Irish, recent immigrants to Manchester and then London. They were gregarious, witty and fun. They also believed in education and sent him to an independent Catholic boys' school in London where the intake was unusually cosmopolitan. There he soon discovered that, loner though he was, humour was a route to popularity. He was also fortunate to have some excellent teachers who taught him to appreciate literature and poetry, French as well as English. School, for Declan, was a good experience, but he left not knowing what he wanted to be or do, although 'I remember seeing theatre and knowing that I wanted to be part of it in some way.'

Both men, curiously, studied law at Cambridge, when they weren't involved in theatre, but only Declan pursued it afterwards for a short while, seeing no future for himself as an actor. Nick went to art school – 'the fee was £15, you couldn't do it now,' – then worked for a while with a theatrical designer in Edinburgh 'who taught me a lot.' After vain attempts to do something in pub theatres, their breakthrough came with a play done for free by experienced actors in the theatre of the old Charing Cross Hospital.

The production was seen by Lyall Jones, the Director of the Arts Education Drama School, who invited them to direct his students in some of their plays. It was their lucky break and, through working with the students, Declan discovered his own director's philosophy: 'They had a need to act better; it was my job to help them to act better. I would watch them and say, why don't I believe it? It's because they don't believe it. I would invent exercises and techniques to help. They seemed to get more confident.'

Then they found their second patron. Ruth Marks of the Arts Council offered them £5000 towards a UK tour if they could find enough theatres to take them. They had no idea how to go about it. They couldn't pay proper rates to the actors, the van they bought by mortgaging their flat they could not afford to MOT or license, and the actors driving it got caught and lost their licences. Administratively, it was all a bit of a disaster, but the plays worked. They were asked to do another tour and were joined by Barbara Matthews who has been their Administrative Director ever since. Cheek by Jowl was on its way. Now, seventeen years later, they are off to reinvent themselves, and to find other ways of doing theatre, starting with Corneille's Le Cid at the Avignon Festival.

'Courage is easy,' Nick says, 'when you are ignorant and have nothing to lose. We got lots of bad advice at the beginning. They told us not to do it. It was the wrong time, they said. We should aim for the middle of the road before we tried to branch out. Luckily we ignored them.' And talent? Declan maintains that curiosity is much more important than creativity, which he considers an overrated word. 'We all know everything, the problem is finding the way to unlock what we know.' For both men the theatre is a way to indulge their curiosity, 'to investigate extreme situations safely'.

As with all the alchemists, the lucky break and the early patrons helped. Their personal partnership was also vital, for alchemy can be lonely: 'We couldn't have done it without each other.' Why did they do it? 'No one would employ us, so we had to do it ourselves!' More seriously, 'Because if I didn't do this I would go mad.' And their parting advice to would-be alchemists: 'Take your work seriously but improvise your career.'

Charles Dunstone

(Carphone Warehouse)

THE PORTRAIT OF CHARLES DUNSTONE IN his home says a lot about him. 'I like the unconventional and doing the unexpected,' he says and not many people have a sculptural spiral staircase running through the middle of their sitting-room. But he is a very 'normal' individual, conventional in appearance, tidy, well-organized and sensible. He is also pictured on the phone, but then mobile phones are at the centre of his life, as founder and Managing Director of Carphone Warehouse, the leading seller of mobile phones in Britain today.

He has, he says, no great personal ambition and that rings true, yet only nine years ago he started the Carphone Warehouse with £6000 of his own savings. Today Charles is Chairman and majority shareholder of a business with 173 outlets in the UK and another hundred in mainland Europe, with 1300 employers, a turnover last year of £171 million and a before-tax profit of £14 million. They have never borrowed or even had an overdraft. He is thirty-three years old.

We can all draw encouragement from the fact that such an unassuming matter-of-fact person can be what is, by any standards, an extraordinarily successful alchemist. 'If you asked people who have known me for a long time I don't think they would say that I was a particularly entrepreneurial person. I am absolutely staggered, myself, at what has happened. But I am also surprised that other people are amazed at what we have done at Carphone Warehouse because it's not particularly amazing. It's all applied common sense, what we do.'

Carphone Warehouse seems to be all that its founder is – low key, determined not to be arrogant, well organized, honest and straightforward but, behind the quiet exterior, unconventional and innovative. Such attitudes usually come from a sure self-confidence, but Charles says that it's actually the other way round. 'I'm not really a confident person. In a strange way the success of the business is due to a *lack* of confidence. I want to be sure that our customers are never disappointed. We never promise what we might not be able to live up to. We play it down. I always want our customers to be surprised by what they get. We have no right to the customers' money. We have to earn it. That's just common sense, not confidence.'

Charles has always taken his own decisions in life. Born into a secure family background, the elder of two children of a BP executive, he went to boarding-school when his parents were posted abroad. There he joined the naughty gang but surprised the school by doing better than expected in his exams and gaining a place at university, only he decided to spend a year first getting a job, ending up as a sales executive with a Cambridge computer company. 'I was having a great time, company car, expense account and so on.' The thought of doing business studies at university in Liverpool did not appeal. 'I was bored with unproductive learning, I wanted to do things, to make things happen.'

He learnt, nevertheless, but productively. The computer company was staffed with young people enthused by the technology. They were producing computers far more sophisticated, and expensive, than the customers needed or wanted. Charles took note, for future use. When the business later changed hands, Charles moved to NEC, the Japanese technology company where he became a sales manager in the fast growing area of mobile phones. He was the first manager under thirty that the company had ever known. When his manager put him up for the job NEC questioned why he had no university degree. 'He has been educated in the University of Life,' the manager replied. The Japanese had never heard of this cliché and were much impressed.

After three years he realized that there was no reason why he couldn't do for himself what he was doing for NEC. He knew the products, the other suppliers and the customers. It cost little to enter the market and the time was right, the era of the personal phone was about to begin. He rented a room in an apartment of office suites and set up on his own with, initially, one colleague and his savings of £6000. In his first year he had a turnover of £1.5 million. From then on 'it just grew', with the first shop opening in 1990. But Charles had learnt from his years in the other businesses and set about applying the 'applied common sense' that he used in his personal life to his fast growing business.

'We treat our people very generously and pay them more than our rivals but in return we expect them to meet our high standards. We invest a lot on their training from the very beginning and we will take anyone on board provided that they have the right attitude.' They won't take on anyone who has worked for another mobile phone company because Charles does not want to import any of the hard-sell practices common in the rest of the industry. Nor does he want his new recruits to learn as they go. 'They are supposed to be serving the customer, not learning. If a customer comes into one of our shops looking for expert advice he or she wants to meet someone who knows the product and can talk knowledgeably about it.' So all new recruits have to go on an eighteen-day training programme with a two-hour test at the end. If they fail they don't get to join.

The staff get paid a commission on sales – but it is the same amount irrespective of the price of the product. That way the customer can be assured that there is no pressure to buy the more expensive model. 'No lunch' is a firm rule, meaning that there are no expense account meals, which Charles feels can only create resentment against those whose role gives them the opportunity, but which can also be a waste of time and can write off the afternoon. As always, he is extending his personal principles into his organization, 'treating the customers and the people as I would want to be treated'. This year he is thinking about those customers who have seen the market price of their phone collapse since they bought it six months ago. They might well be feeling aggrieved. Thinking of how he would like to be treated, he is planning to send them a voucher for the difference. It's only applied common sense.

To what does he attribute his success? 'Partly luck. Being in the right place at the right time. If I've got any special talent it is that I may be more sensitive than others. I try to understand what people want and how they like to be treated.' He has a fierce belief that there is good in everyone and that 'no one comes to work to do a bad job'. It is up to him as manager-in-chief to make sure that each member of his company has a chance to show his or her talents and to develop them. Once again, his personal attitudes and values infect his business. Those who are true to themselves in public as well as private enjoy a powerful form of integrity.

The future must hold many options for this understated alchemist but for the moment his passion is focused on where he is: 'I have such high standards and aims for the business that it's going to be a long time until it lives up to them all.'

Rose Fenton and Lucy Neal

(London International Festival of Theatre)

IN 1980, FRESH OUT OF WARWICK University where they first met, Rose and Lucy decided that the London theatre scene needed the injection of some more international talent and that they were the people to do it. They set about creating the first London International Festival of Theatre (LIFT), which was launched the next summer. Every second summer since then LIFT has lit up London with its astonishing programmes of work from abroad. Both now married, with growing families, these two women are an example of how demanding alchemy can be combined with a fulfilling family life, although the balance is never easy and requires much understanding and support from the other partner in the marriage. They agree that 'my family is my foundation. It puts things into perspective.'

Rose and Lucy started by roving the world looking at theatrical companies to invite to the festival. Today they also commission new works; they pioneer creative participatory events including, in 1997, a breath-taking piece of fire theatre in Battersea Park, by Christopher Berthonneau, the world's leading pyrotechnician, and the pupils of Stockwell Park School in London, together with 7000 members of the public. 'One of the things we asked ourselves', explains Rose, 'was "How do you create new rituals for a secular age?" Participating in an exhilarating work like *Un Peu Plus de Lumière* and being part of a huge crowd of people moving across the park is perhaps one way of answering that need.'

LIFT, in short, is endlessly inventive. The two women have explored the use of new spaces for theatre – the River Thames, the empty corridors of an abandoned hotel, a Soho street, an empty warehouse – and have made a point of involving local schools, starting with a joint project at the National Maritime Museum in 1993 in which six Greenwich schools, Emergency Exit Arts and the Vietnam Refugee Centre created *Sang Song,* an open-air extravaganza alongside the dazzling Hanoi Water Puppets. Since then every festival has involved local schoolchildren in some of its productions and in 1996, a non-festival year, a whole range of projects were created in which artists worked with schools for the mini-festival Out of Lift, which was so successful that it won a Prudential Award for the Arts.

Rose and Lucy believe passionately that theatre is more than entertainment. Inspirational, celebratory, provocative and passionate, it helps us to make sense of the world, to explore ideas, feelings and arguments. 'Theatre is the place to say what's important,' Rose maintains. 'There is wonderment wherever you are,' adds Lucy and she wants everyone to sense it. Theatre, to them, is educational in the broadest and most exciting sense of that word and, at its best, can change individuals and society. 'Everybody needs to engage with their creativity.'

To make it all happen Rose and Lucy must effectively create a new organization of some seventy people every two years with a turnover of nearly £2 million, raise the money, enlist the support of a hundred or so sponsors, choose and invite the participating companies, find the venues, organize travel and accommodation, manage the promotion, entertainment and hospitality that are crucial to the success of each festival. It demands a biennial piece of organizational alchemy. That it has worked so well for ten festivals is entirely due to the inspiration and drive of these two women who have not only started something refreshingly new but have continued to run it, develop it and learn from it.

They couldn't, they say, have done it without each other. 'We give each other confidence and can take greater risks. And then you look as if you are having fun, doing it together. That's terribly important for the rest of the team to see.' By combining their talents, 'You can make sure that you are playing off the best foot' because, they say, they are completely different people in many ways. Maybe alchemy in double harness can be more fun and more successful.

They first met in theatre at Warwick. Both were in love with drama and with travel, although neither seriously thought of acting as a career. One vacation they were encouraged to bring a group of actors to perform at a festival in Portugal. Their production was a disaster but the festival itself was an eye-opener. 'That's what we want to do,' they realized instantly, 'run an international festival of theatre.' It offered a way of combining their two passions: theatre and travel.

Not that they were strangers to either. Rose had had an unconventional childhood. Her parents owned a dilapidated stately home in Yorkshire. When money ran out, as it did every year, they rented it to rich

Americans and took off with their four children in a van to explore Greece and central Europe on £1 a day. They missed out on school but in its place learnt a lot about people and about resourcefulness. 'I realized that it was possible to communicate across language barriers and I was touched by the generosity of ordinary people who were complete strangers.'

Lucy grew up in an equally unusual environment – Eton College where her father was a housemaster. 'Slightly subversive' about the traditions of such a place, she treated it as an adventure playground, a place to play with roles. 'There was something exciting happening every moment. I was always looking for adventure,' she remembers. At Bedales, later, she was forced by the tradition there to work out who she was in order to survive. It was to stand her in good stead when she failed to get accepted for university. She then bullied her way into an interview with Warwick, studied English and Italian in order to indulge what by now was her addiction to travel and had 'four years of Italian adventures – that was my degree'.

Lucy's father's career at Eton was cut short when his attempts to change some aspects of the school fell foul of the then headmaster. His treatment by his superiors at that time taught her that 'if you want to change something you have to take it into your own hands and stick to your principles'. It's no use relying on others. Rose, having initially been embarrassed by her unconventional parents, realized, in her teens, that they were admired and even almost envied by her peers, and 'my parents never questioned what I did. They believed that each person has to find her own way. I was accepted for what I was, unconditionally.'

Recently Lucy discovered that they had both had unconventional great-aunts who had, by a strange coincidence, once produced a musical pageant together in the grounds of Madresfield Court in Worcestershire. Perhaps the seeds of alchemy were in their genes all along.

Sabrina Guinness

(Youth Culture TV)

SABRINA GUINNESS IS PICTURED IN THE studios of YCTV, the project which she dreamt up and launched five years ago. YCTV stands for Youth Culture Television. It takes young people aged eleven to nineteen and trains them in every aspect of television work, culminating in the production of a half-hour programme every week, which is played on cable television three times a day throughout the week. In the photograph she is seen with some of the Kids Club, the under-elevens who hope one day to become full members. The enthusiasm in the room is infectious.

This is education for reality, designed principally for young people who are disillusioned by traditional schooling. Whether or not they end up with a job in the media they leave, says Sabrina, believing in themselves, with enhanced self-discipline and a set of practical and personal skills, which will always stand them in good stead. It is serious stuff. Anyone applying has first to go through a four-day induction course. This is followed by a series of technical workshops. Only then do they get to work on the actual programmes for broadcasting.

On the day we first met they were preparing for an interview with Chris Smith, the Minister for Culture, Media and Sport. This was to be the start of a series of *Pass the Microphone* in which each interviewee would invite the next guest and ask the first question. Devised by the young people themselves it would, they hoped, be the first programme to be screened on mainstream television. Luke was the one chosen to interview the minister. He had left school at fourteen. 'They gave up on me,' he said and had gladly agreed that he should attend YCTV instead. Now seventeen he has the maturity and confidence of someone much older and, in preparation for the interview with the minister, has immersed himself for the first time in the world and language of politics.

The current membership of YCTV stands at 380 young people and ten schools collaborate with the project. It costs £330,000 a year to run, which currently has to be raised from foundations or businesses. Sabrina dreams of the day when there will be a dedicated YCTV channel, not just in Britain but throughout the world. 'It could alter the lives of many hundreds of young people.' The voice of teenagers needs to be heard, she argues. 'And isn't it better to fit education to the individual than slotting the individual into the education?'

She is speaking from personal experience. Born into a conventional middle-class branch of a family with a well-known name, the second of a pair of twins, she was given what was, at the time, the standard education for girls. 'My first school did not do A Levels. We learnt to arrange flowers and to cook.' Asked to leave her next school, she went to Switzerland and eventually trained as a Montessori teacher. 'I never had any clear ambition. I supposed that I would marry, settle in the country and have children.' In the event she did none of these things. Instead, she went to California at the age of eighteen, as the nanny for Tatum O'Neal who had just won an Oscar for her part in *Paper Moon*.

'America changed my life. It opened things up and made anything possible. In America you are what you are, not where you come from.' In California she met people from very different backgrounds for the first time, as well as the English diaspora of the time, including a lot of famous names who introduced her to the world of movies where she started working in development, taking a script and giving it life. 'I discovered that I loved putting ideas and people together.' Her rather empty education had left her curious and her shyness evaporated in the freedom of Los Angeles. 'America allowed me to escape and to get to know myself.'

The Los Angeles riots opened her eyes even wider. Many people retreated behind their steel gates but some reached out to the teenagers, bringing members of the different gangs together to write music and dramas about their experience, 'improvising in a safe place'. But she was thirty-eight; time, she felt, to return to Britain because, exhilarating though it was, in the end Los Angeles, she found, had no soul. Back in London she talked with Barney Platt-Mills who was training young people to make videos. Great, she thought, but why not *do* something with the videos? Within a month she had homed in on the idea of YCTV, rung Greg Dyke, whom she had never met, persuaded him to be chairman of the project, formed her charity, found premises and was open for business. American hustle had come to Britain. 'A lot of people told me that it was a mad idea, but I think that we have proved ourselves.'

But why should this very competent woman, who could clearly do almost anything she put her mind to, want to devote the prime of her life to this project? 'I really love it. It helps a lot of people. It's fun. It's creative. I like living on the edge and I like the diversity of my life, working here all day, then dressing up and going out to a completely different world in the evening.' She had also been scarred by her early experience of being known only for the famous names that she had been associated with – from Warren Beatty and Mick Jagger to Prince Charles. 'It was absolutely awful. It makes you feel you're nothing; to be known just because you've gone out with someone.' From then on she decided that she would be known for her achievements, not her friends.

She says she was lucky. It started twenty years ago when she met Ryan O'Neal while playing frisbee with friends on Parson's Green. But there were others there that day; only Sabrina made the contact. There were several young Englishwomen in Hollywood in those days but only Sabrina used her contacts to put something back into society. Her Guinness surname was a disadvantage in childhood – 'I used to pretend that I lived in the basement of our big house, which you could see from my school' – but, she admits, can be useful these days in opening doors. And, thanks to Hollywood, 'I've met enough famous people not to be fazed or impressed by anyone.'

As for early influences: 'I didn't really know my parents when I was young, but there was a cousin who made films and was quite a rebel. He was an influence, I suppose. I never wanted to conform. To regret not doing something is far worse than to regret something you have done. As for school, I didn't do anything really creative – sad really. I'm sure that I could have learnt to play the piano but the piano teacher was German and could speak no English. In support, I do have my gang of siblings. All five of us were born within five years so we are very close. Having no children of my own I can enjoy being an aunt.'

Now forty-four, Sabrina Guinness is determined to see YCTV become not only self-financing but a model for the rest of the world. 'I'm looking for a major sponsor, preferably from the world of broadcasting, possibly from America, and I want more government support.' It seems very likely that she will succeed for she has consistently kept faith with her own maxim: 'Follow your heart and grab your luck.'

Philip Hughes
(Painter and Logica)

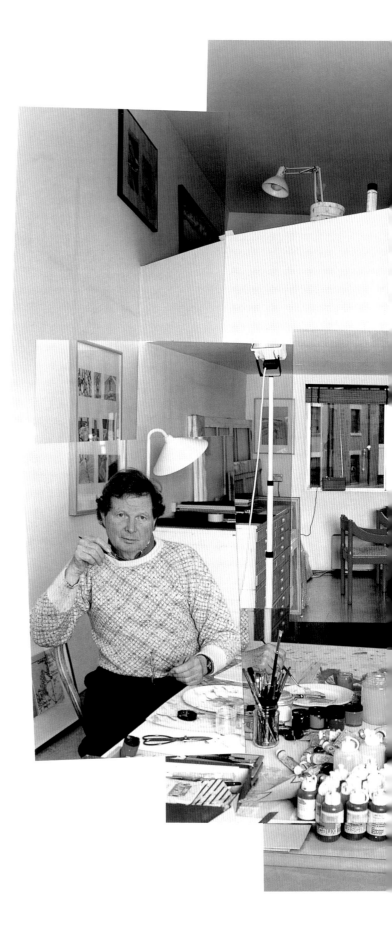

PHILIP HUGHES IS TODAY AN ARTIST and a very successful one. His 'formative landscapes' sell for many thousands of pounds, as do his original jewellery designs, while his exhibitions range the world. Most recently one has toured Australia. In this way Hughes is a pure alchemist, creating paintings and objects of beauty out of nothing except his imagination. Central to his approach to landscape is a preoccupation with its geology, the bones beneath its surface.

For those who find his original works too expensive his *Notebooks*, recently published by Thames and Hudson, offer an exciting introduction to his work. From Iceland to Australia, Philip captures the exquisite essence of a landscape or, at the other extreme, the tracks and traceries of a leaf or a piece of bark, seeing beyond and beneath the familiar to the very signature of being. He has been called an 'aerialist of the imagination' and a 'cartographer of the nature of things'.

Back in London, he works in his Camden studio, with its small office upstairs, a private world which he leaves only to be with his family or, as glimpsed in the photograph, to pursue his other role as Chairman of the Trustees of the National Gallery. That role is his, however, largely because of his earlier existence, as Chairman of a billion-pound company, Logica, the computer technology firm that Philip and his colleague Len Taylor created from nothing thirty years ago. He resigned as Chairman in 1990 after twenty years and now has no formal connection with them. As a piece of business alchemy, Logica must count as one of the most successful in recent British history. Starting in 1969, when computing was in its infancy, Philip and his colleagues first put to use much of the technology which has made the Internet possible today. He can justifiably be called one of the architects of the information age.

It is not often that one finds someone practising alchemy so successfully in two such very different fields. Few can hope for Philip's combination of talents but he stands out as a striking example of how an individual can cram two lives into one, how the creative impulse can work in very different ways in different spheres and how it is possible, even desirable, to leave one form of success behind while there is still time and energy to develop and enjoy another. Who knows what seeds of alchemy lurk in all of us? It is never too late to try another life.

Not that Philip Hughes looked like an alchemist at first. A bright lad at his Bedford school, he went to Cambridge with a scholarship to read engineering, then joined Shell as a sales engineer and went out for his first tour of duty in Malaysia. But such a straightforward career was not for him: 'I knew by the end of the first five days that I didn't belong there, but it took me four years to get out.' Cambridge had changed him. He went there as a conventional public schoolboy. He emerged as a committed Labour Party supporter, with an awakening interest in painting. He also switched from engineering to economics, where his original flair for mathematics found an outlet. Shell provided a way to get to Australia where his family had moved five years before without him. An odd reason, perhaps, for a career choice, but from it Philip learnt at least two lessons: that large organizations were not to his taste and that he was a mathematician not an engineer. To know what you are not is often a first step to discovering what you really want to be or do.

Back in London, unemployed having resigned from Shell, he stumbled on a book about computing – an almost unknown topic then. 'It was a flash of light. I knew immediately what I wanted to do.' Chance continued to play its part. Passing a shop window he discovered that it belonged to a small software consulting company, one of the first of its kind, called CEIR (later SCICON). Philip calls it chance, but his eyes were already open for it. If you know what you are looking for the opportunities often leap out at you. With his smattering of management experience he quickly ascended the small hierarchy in SCICON, only to find it purchased by BP who wanted it for their own purposes, not for the pioneering route which Philip preferred. He went looking for other jobs but none was on offer from the competitors who found him overqualified.

'So I had no choice but to start my own business. A bad model for an entrepreneur, I'm afraid!' he laughs. But many stumble into alchemy because all other routes are closed to them and they refuse to give up their dreams. If you know what you want to do, you have to do it, come what may. The next few years were exciting and successful. The business grew fast. Life was busy, full and fun. Meanwhile, Philip the artist had not been idle. There were enough works to exhibit in a shared show with Beryl Bainbridge in 1972. Philip then did an extraordinary thing. Six

133

years into the exhilarating ride with his new company, he took a full year off to paint. He was forty. It was time to test whether his art was serious. Was he good enough?

That sabbatical was a turning point. He went back to Logica. 'I owed it to the shareholders and to my colleagues who had been extra-ordinarily generous in letting me go. Besides I loved the work.' But five years later, asked to complete his entry for *Who's Who*, he gave 'artist' as his occupation and gradually thereafter began to scale down his time with the company and to devote more to his painting, finally resigning as Chairman in 1990 and from the Board in 1995. 'It's like bringing up a child,' he says. 'One day, they have their own identity and you have to let them go.'

Philip claims that he stumbled into entrepreneurship and alchemy, but there were some pointers from the beginning. He discovered inde-pendence at an early age, when his family emigrated to Australia. He had no choice but to look after himself in the holidays, with no one to con-fide in, no one to decide things for him. He doesn't remember thinking himself unusual, or feeling lonely, but the experience increased his self-reliance, the willingness to go it alone if need be.

Unusually, too, he had no teacher nor mentor for his art. Self-taught, he developed his own unique style, although he worshipped the work of Ben Nicholson, whose paintings were a major influence early on. Inde-pendence, combined with the desire to take charge of their own life, is characteristic of many alchemists. They are not organization people, unless the organization is theirs. They regard the control of time as vital – hence Philip's decision to take the sabbatical year, and the deliberate allocation of time between his painting and his business role. 'Nothing is more important than time' says Philip, 'but it is the most difficult issue for creative people, for their time is often at the expense of their family or other responsibilities.' As a double alchemist, Philip Hughes has had to make himself a master of his time. The results are there for all to see.

Andy Law

(St Luke's Advertising Agency)

ANDY LAW IS PICTURED AT THE heart of his creation – St Luke's advertising agency off the Euston Road in London. He would say that it wasn't his creation alone; thirty-four brave souls came with him. But brave souls need someone to lead them and that leader was Andy. Not many people with a young family would throw up a high-status job, with all the perks, salary and bonuses, to create something that they believed in, but Andy did just that, twice.

Everything about St Luke's is unusual, starting with the name. Most advertising agencies are named after their founders or owners, subsequently reduced to initials, like CDP where Andy first made his name. But everyone at St Luke's is an owner, all hundred of them now, so that clearly wouldn't work. St Luke, moreover, is the patron saint of creativity and of healing, a combination pleasingly appropriate to St Luke's, which Andy likes to see as a place where all problems are solved.

The sole office visible in the photograph, upstairs, has the name of a client above the door. That's because the only private rooms in the place are kitted out as theme rooms for their clients. Everyone else works where they can find a perch, in one of the many available work areas around the building, which was originally a warehouse and still retains the same structure. Meetings take place wherever, often standing up, as in the photograph. When they come in to work everyone picks up their mobile phone, which has been charging on a rack overnight, and that's the only way to find them, by dialling them and asking where they are.

It looks chaotic to anyone used to the rows of cells that make up the typical office building, but creativity springs from chaos and St Luke's is creative all right. After only two years of existence it won the prized accolade of Agency of the Year. St Luke's is not only an unusual desk-free working environment, a sort of creative clubhouse, it is a whole new philosophy of management, fascinatingly described in Andy's book about it all – *Open Minds,* published in 1998 by Orion in Britain and Wiley in America as *Creative Company*.

Advertising agencies should, by definition, be creative environments, but in fact they are usually rather conventional places, devoted to wealth creation for themselves as much as to advertising creation for their clients. That can be a sort of gilded prison, as Andy discovered when he was a director of one of the most prestigious agencies. He was well on the way to becoming extremely rich in his thirties. 'But I was just being a "businessman"', he says, 'not myself.'

So when Chiat Day, one of the few really experimental agencies in America, invited him to leave and help set up a new agency for them in London, with no perks and nothing guaranteed, he didn't hesitate, even though he had to leave all his share options behind. 'I went from the corner office to an orange box,' is how he describes it. It was his first chance to do something he believed in, to construct a place that worked for the good of all, not just the shareholders, a place of fun as well as of creativity and excellence.

Despite the inevitable ups and downs they made a great success of it over the next three years, even outdoing their American parent in their zany creative ways. Then one morning the phone rang while Andy was still in his pyjamas. It was Jay Chiat in Vancouver. 'We've sold the company,' he said. He had, too, to a colossus improbably called Omnicom and Andy was offered the second top job in the London agency. It was one more chance to enter the gilded prison and once again Andy had no doubts. Meeting his potential new colleagues for the first time he looked at them and thought, 'I wouldn't even employ you, let alone work for you.' We have all felt that at times but most of us have lacked the resolution to do anything about it.

But Andy turned disaster into opportunity and persuaded the rest of the old Chiat Day company in London to join him in founding a new type of organization, soon to be called St Luke's. It was a scary time, but exciting to have to live your dream. He was thirty-eight.

Andy was brought up in a children's home so antiquated that it was still called a home for Waifs and Strays, as he revealed to all his staff at one away-day gathering. 'I told everyone that my real father was Indian and my mother English, and that they were teen lovers. I told them how painfully embarrassed I'd been all my life about this and how I had feigned an Italian background. I told them how I had been adopted at three by my new parents, that my father was rector of Battersea and how I grew up in a series of vicarages.'

139

He could also have told them how a classics master at his Grammar school first convinced him that he was clever, and reinforced his love of books and poetry, how his parents drummed the concept of 'fairness' into their brood of very diverse adopted children (Andy was the second eldest) and how this had become a driving force in his philosophy of life, how he devoured Jules Verne's books of invention as a child and how he will always remember being allowed to stay up late to watch Neil Armstrong take his first steps on the moon.

All these influences and seeds of alchemy were to surface later on. But Andy was perhaps lucky in that his talents allowed him to taste the glitter of life early on, in those glory days of the big agency, and to see it for what it was, blood money of a sort. That done and crossed off the list, he could get on with his real life. Ultimately, he says, he wants to earn the right to have on his tombstone the words, 'He made a difference.'

The dedication of his book reveals what drives him, and keeps him sane. It reads:

> *To my parents, Peter and Audrey, who taught me fairness.*
> *To my wife, Amanda, who keeps me on my toes (especially*
> *when my head is in the clouds)*
> *and to my children, Tom, Olivia and Venetia, who assume that all*
> *places of work are like St Luke's.*

One suspects that Andy's next mission will be to try to make sure that their assumption comes true. St Luke's, he says, is now a movement and movements should spread.

Martin Leach

(Magazine Publisher)

IN 1988, AGED THIRTY-FOUR, MARTIN LEACH was down and out in London, with bailiffs knocking at the door. He was far from home in New Zealand and needed work and money – fast. The track record thus far was not encouraging: left school at sixteen with one O level, a succession of short jobs in New Zealand, Australia and Britain – 'I wasn't what you might call a company man!' – and one failed business venture in Sydney. The future was unpromising. 'A ship without a rudder' one employer had called him.

Today, ten years later, Martin is the justifiably proud proprietor of his own publishing company, which he started with a £3000 loan from a supportive bank manager. He has three flourishing magazines and two more about to be launched. In his new offices, where the front cover of his flagship magazine, *Human Resources*, welcomes the visitor and a bottle of New Zealand wine is never far away, Martin employs thirty busy people, manages a revenue of £2.5 million and takes comfort in a pre-tax profit this year of £300,000. This, however, is just the beginning, he says. In fact, since this portrait was made, *Human Resources* has been sold, releasing more funds for new projects.

It wasn't as if Martin knew anything about publishing. His odd jobs had been just that – odd. The failed business venture, in which he had a ten per cent stake, was a clever idea for cut-price tickets for Australians travelling the world. It was a wild success at first, but then collapsed when one of the main airlines involved went bankrupt, leaving Martin, who was by then looking after the London end, destitute. He knew, however, that he could deliver the goods and, in particular, that he was an excellent salesman. So, as a stop-gap in 1998, he started selling advertising space.

An advertising salesman, no matter how successful, is not an alchemist and by now Martin knew that he wanted to start and do his own thing. He was not comfortable being anyone's hired help, no matter how financially rewarding in the short term. As he went on his rounds he spotted what he felt was a gap in a growing market. The world of what was called 'human resources' was inadequately served, he reckoned, by the few available magazines. He was sure that he could do better. The early market research was not encouraging – everyone he spoke to told him that it wouldn't work, that executives didn't read and that if they did enough material was already available.

Like most alchemists, Martin thrives on being challenged, provided his own analysis suggests that the challenge can be met. He decided, despite the warnings, to become a publisher, which meant finding an editor, a printer and a market. His first attempt nearly resulted in a fatal lawsuit when a photograph sited out of context appeared to libel a major organization. Martin had checked the magazine after it had been printed instead of before. He closed it down before the case came to court, wrote it off to experience and started again. Set-backs don't deter if you know what you want and believe in yourself. The rest is recent history.

Martin's story is a great encouragement to all those people who find themselves still lost for a career in their mid-thirties. 'Don't worry about your twenties' says Martin. 'They are for mucking around, finding out about yourself.' In his mid-thirties, things began to come together as Martin realized what he was good at and what he liked doing. But only in his forties did it all start to happen. 'There's no need to hurry,' he reckons.

Martin is now looking ahead to his fifties, a time when, he says, he would like to give something back, using the financial base that he will by then have built up. Money isn't the point of his existence, he maintains, 'but I have never ever had any financial security in my whole life. Once I have that then I feel that I can stretch myself in other worlds.' Martin would like to explore his growing interests in new ways of living by turning those interests into businesses. He has in mind, among other things, the establishment of a healing centre, both in the physical and the spiritual sense, a place for suffering souls to find peace and health.

That is a very different sort of world. But Martin, a true alchemist, is quickly bored, particularly by success. 'I am always discontented' he says. 'I'm always looking over the hill for something better.' When one magazine is up and running, start a new one for a different audience. When one career is thriving, chuck it in and begin another, one perhaps more true to yourself at that stage of life. 'As I get older I feel that I can be more myself. In the past, work was money, nowadays work is me. And I like starting things.'

Being a Kiwi, an outsider in the traditional world of Britain, helped him develop his ideas. As such you can more easily define yourself, you can't be placed neatly in a slot, except one of being 'different' and Martin, one suspects, rather enjoys being different: it is easier to fail, learn from the experience and start again, because no one who matters to you is noticing. It undoubtedly helped that in his family of six children (he was the third baby but the first boy) he was his mother's favourite. She died when he was in his twenties but he still feels that he is in touch with her. 'My mother would be proud of me now, I think.'

That initial success in the Sydney ticketing business gave him the kind of start he needed. At some time in the first third of our lives we need to know that we are good – at something. For some it happens at school or college, particularly if they meet exceptional teachers; for others it is a matter of luck. After the Sydney venture Martin knew that he was OK. It was then just a question of finding the right outlet for his talents.

Now that he is up and running Martin is determined to keep on learning. He has chosen a chairman who 'makes me feel awkward', he has joined a club of entrepreneurs who mentor each other, he is always asking people how he is doing. Maybe it helped him that he managed to do so little learning at school. He has now taken the 'school of experience' more seriously than many who have been encouraged by early scholastic success to think that they know it all, or that they can always mug it up.

'I know where I am going now, but it has taken a long time,' he says.

Mapi Lucchesi

(Lucchesi – Translation Business)

MAPI LUCCHESI IS PICTURED IN HER new and as yet unfinished home near London's Hyde Park with her baby and her partner Michael, while she gets on with her work, infant over her arm. The work is the management of a translation and voice-over business which uses the skills of 1500 translators and actors. The business, which she started and which bears her name, is now fourteen years old and has a turnover of more than £1 million. It all belongs to Mapi. She is thirty-five.

The company does translations for businesses, their brochures, technical literature, in-house newsletters and videos which can each need to be translated into over twenty different languages. Then there are subtitles and/or voice-overs for films, animations, corporate videos, all of which need native-language actors to speak the translations. Actors are also needed to read tapes for the hard of hearing and interpreters are wanted for international conferences. It is going to be a long time before everyone can speak English and until it happens globalization can only mean an expanding market for Lucchesi's services. Her clients span the globe but the majority are based in the UK 'because it is easier to collect the money'.

There are, however, some inherent problems. Mapi's most precious asset is her database, her list of translators and actors catalogued by language, competencies and availability. She soon realized that it wasn't difficult for anyone to copy this data when she was away and leave her to start his or her own firm. She now retains a very small group of trusties in the office – only five in all, and none of them likely to want to break away. More crucial still are her client contacts, which she cultivates herself with great care. Such personal control is hard work and Mapi confesses that it is only recently that she has had time to concentrate on her life away from the office, 'but babies can't wait'.

How did it all happen? 'By mistake' she says, laughing. Mapi Lucchesi was born near Lucca in Tuscany in Italy, the second child of a middle-class Tuscan family. Her father was an industrial designer with, she says, 'no idea about business – he even sold our house for the wrong price'. Her mother was a traditional Italian matriarch, 'beautiful and wonderful but her life was the home and the family'. That was not Mapi's idea of what her own life should be although, as the only daughter, she came under great pressure to do the traditional thing: marriage to a local boy followed by children and ultimately grandchildren. She was, however, her grandmother's descendant and grandmother, she says, was a frustrated businesswoman with a lot of common sense and a great understanding of people – 'which is what business is all about.'

Business must have been in her bloodstream somehow. When she was eight the family went on a visit to Volterra, the home of alabaster. She saw these lovely little white stones lying around everywhere. She picked them up and persuaded her elder brother to help her sell them to the villagers when they got home for 50 or 100 lire each. Her brother, she says, was a beautiful small boy so she used to approach visiting film companies and offer him as an extra, keeping half of the money for herself. Enrolled at Pisa University to study languages, she made sure that she got a job in a bank at the same time, but banking, particularly Italian banking, was not, she soon realized, the kind of occupation that held any attractions for her.

Providentially, she was sent to London when she was twenty to sell her uncle's precious cello. She already knew then that languages (she spoke five) and travel were going to shape her life. She loved London and resolved to come back as soon as she had finished her degree, even though her school English, she quickly noted, was Shakespearean and barely understood – 'We shall depart, so fare thee well' she would say, rather than 'goodbye.' Back in London she got work with a translation service in Mayfair but when it became clear to her that the translation was a front for rather more dubious activities she left. One of her clients, however, asked her to continue doing their work. 'Why not?' she thought, 'and why not add one or two more clients while I am at it?'

She persuaded her bank manager to lend her £2000 to buy a computer and a filing cabinet – 'He trusted me; English bankers are wonderful!' Her grandfather gave her £3000 as a deposit on a flat, she had £50 of her own and a kitchen table, which was her office desk. It was enough. She knew what she could do and what clients wanted. 'Selling is exciting. You've got to work out what attracts them. You have perhaps fifteen minutes to get someone interested. If you see their faces go blank you have to change your approach at once.'

It was successful from the beginning. 'I like languages so I liked my product and some clients, Amnesty International for example, did really interesting and valuable work. In the beginning I wasn't bothered about money. But I realized that people were hanging around me because they saw that I was a little pot of cash.' She had to get real, keeping things close to her chest, trusting few, sticking to her principles. 'If you work only for money, you don't care. If you aim for quality maybe you have fewer clients but you keep them. It doesn't excite me much to make another £50,000. I like buying things but I've got enough. If you have too much you lose the excitement.'

Mapi says that she loves imitating things. 'There is nothing more exciting than starting something when you don't know what is going to happen. The trouble is that once you have started a business you have to run it.' One senses that she is becoming bored by what she now knows so well how to do. So she sets herself goals and deadlines for her future. In five years' time she would like to sell the firm and move on. The problem is that much of the heart of the business is in her head. Somehow she has to systematize her knowledge, get it out of her head so that others can use it when she is no longer around.

Then what? Her architect brother is building a house for her near Lucca and she would like to have two more children but it seems very unlikely that she will revert to being a Tuscan mum. Her own mother has come to recognize that Mapi is only happy when she is running something. On a recent visit to see her, her mother said, 'I can see that you're at your happiest in your office with a lot of chaos around.' But writing is one of Mapi's unfulfilled needs. She wrote a lot of poetry when she was young and would love now to write film scripts, but they would have to be based on reality, not fantasy. Words and people are her real fascination. She has made them into one successful venture. There seems nothing to stop this bubbling inquiring personality from turning them into another.

What, looking back, has driven her? 'I love learning a lot and in life I think that's the best thing.' 'You walk so fast,' her mother complained once, trying to keep up with her.

'But there is so much to do,' Mapi replied.

Jayesh Manek
(Investment Management)

YOU REACH THE SIMPLE, RATHER SPARTAN offices of Manek Investments by going into the Dallas Pharmacy in Ruislip High Street and up to the first floor. It must be one of the more unusual places to find a fund manager but it makes sense when you know that the shop also belongs to Jayesh Manek. Manek was a successful and innovative owner of a string of chemist shops before he won the *Sunday Times* fantasy investment competition not once, but twice, beating 40,000 people, including some of the City's smartest financial brains. He launched the Manek Growth Fund at the end of 1997 and in the first six months had attracted over £80 million from 22,000 investors in forty different countries and had seen its value increase by twenty-two per cent compared with the FTSE All Share Index rise of fourteen per cent. Despite a dip in the autumn of 1998 when the whole stock-market declined sharply, by July 1999 he had over £100 million under management and was showing an increase of 20% overall.

That's a lot of alchemy – particularly having started as a pharmacist. But the signs were there from the time his parents sent him from Uganda to England at the age of fifteen, in 1971, to go to school in Leicester where his two brothers had gone before him. The parents followed a year later, escaping from the despotic rule of Idi Amin, and settled in London where he and his brothers joined them. Family is important in this story. His brother Hasu, originally a graphic designer, works with him in the business and their families share a house. A close family can see you through all sorts of changes, be they from Uganda to England or from pharmacy to investment management.

In Uganda bright boys studied science, so he was destined for some sort of scientific career, possibly in medicine. But he was also a Gujarati and Gujaratis are traders. Pharmacy allowed him to combine science and business so he went to study it in Brighton, became a qualified pharmacist and worked for a time with the large firms as a manager. 'But', he says, 'while I was at college I was actually more interested in stocks and shares than pharmacy,' encouraged by another family member, an uncle this time, who shared his fascination.

Would-be alchemists don't like working for others for long. Looking around, Jayesh saw a gap in the market. Pharmacies in the seventies were either tiny shops off the high street or big emporia like Boots. There was nothing in between. In 1980 he bought a disused freezer store and converted it into a large, bright and friendly chemist's, calling it *Dallas* because that show was dominating the TV screens at the time. 'When you go to a pharmacy,' he says, 'you are often feeling unwell. You want a bright, friendly, cheerful place, not a gloomy little den.' He didn't get much encouragement: 'Freezers into pharmacy will never work,' one journal said and Barclays turned down his application for a loan. But Brian Larcombe of the venture capitalists 3I (ICFC) liked the idea and 'scribbled an offer on a bit of paper and pushed it across the table'. Jayesh Manek has never forgotten. ICFC wanted equity and Jayesh wasn't giving any of that away but Unichem, the wholesaler, guaranteed financial backing and he was off.

The pharmacy worked. He then franchised the idea – 'I was the first into pharmacy franchising,' he says with a smile, and later he was the first into non-dispensing pharmacies when the government tightened the rules on dispensing. All his ideas have since been copied but his chain of pharmacies were the pioneers. The Dallas chain continues but in 1990 he appointed an operations manager, leaving himself free to concentrate on strategy and on his growing interest in stocks and shares. He was ready to test his acumen when the *Sunday Times* launched its first fantasy competition in 1994.

The aim was to manage a notional £10-million portfolio selected from a list of 250 UK quoted shares, both big and small. You had to chose a maximum of ten and within the six months of the competition you were allowed to trade a maximum of thirteen times. The rules were complex and Jayesh played them astutely, turning his £10 million into £502 million by the end of the six months. They tightened the rules the following year but Jayesh still came out top, collecting some respectable prize money each time to fund his real personal portfolio.

Then he got a letter out of the blue from Sir John Templeton, the Bahamas-based investment legend and sponsor of the Templeton prize for religion, and much else besides. John Templeton asked Jayesh Manek to manage £5 million of his personal funds for him. Jayesh replied that he had never looked after anyone else's money and was reluctant to take on the responsibility. Besides, he had been offered jobs by several big City finance houses. Soon afterwards they met for the first time. Jayesh was impressed, not only by Templeton's financial expertise which was widely acknowledged, but by the spiritual quality of the man who, at eighty-four years old, was involved in a host of charities around the world and was dedicating his life to benefiting others. A year after he started to manage the £5 million, Sir John added another £5 million and advised Jayesh that if he wanted to manage a fund he should start his own.

With Templeton's support and together with his brother Hasu, Jayesh Manek decided to take the plunge. He was nervous; perhaps the responsibility of other people's money would make him too cautious. The *Sunday Times* competition was about short-term trading and was only a game after all. He was now going to undertake medium-term investment. The two were very different. To borrow Templeton's motto, it would now be time not timing that mattered, as well as the fundamental strength of the companies Jayesh chose to invest in, ones he could understand. Here, he believes, his background in running his own business gives him an edge. He knows what to look for beyond and behind the figures.

How does he account for his success, so far, in life? He is a Hindu and a man of deep beliefs. 'If you are on the right path, things inevitably fall into place. You do all that you can and you must then leave it to the one above.' Fund management is what he does but 'you can't measure everything with the ruler of money'. Perhaps that is why his staff at the pharmacy don't leave. He admires John Templeton for his humility in spite of his success, for his attention to detail and for his insistence that whatever you do should be for the benefit of others. He has made this philosophy his own and it shines through all that he says and does.

Jayesh has been fortunate, as he would admit, fortunate in the timing of his different ventures, fortunate in the people he met who helped him at crucial stages, but he earned his good fortune by diligence and application. His personal philosophy gives him the strength to do what he believes in and what you believe in you often turn out to be good at. He sees fund management as the responsibility of assisting people by looking after their money and, talking with him, you have no doubt that the thing that drives him is the chance of helping others.

Andrew Mawson

(Bromley-by-Bow Centre and Community Action Network – CAN)

160

IN 1970, AGED SIXTEEN, ANDREW MAWSON was an apprentice with what was then the GPO, having left school with six O levels, bored with education.

Twenty-five years later the Reverend Andrew Mawson was asked by Cardinal Hume and the senior Church leaders of London to organize a Great Banquet in which 30,000 Londoners from all walks of life dined together one night in 200 centres across London. A focus of this unusual and imaginative event was a dinner at the Banqueting House in Whitehall where the great and the good shared a meal with the good but far from great. It was a dramatic piece of alchemy, but based on something even more unusual and more enduring.

The purpose was to encourage Londoners to talk about the future of their communities, using as an example the Bromley-by-Bow Centre created by Andrew out of a decaying church in the East End of London, a centre which is now the admired model around the world for community partnership and regeneration. That church is still the centre, as Andrew feels it has to be and as the portrait shows, but it now includes a Healthy Living Centre, a £1.5 million facility, designed, built and owned by local people and staffed by the National Health Service. Opened by the Health Minister Tessa Jowell in March 1998, it is the first of 300 Healthy Living Centres planned for Britain. The portrait also shows Andrew with the children of the nursery school and some women from the multicultural activities of the centre. There was not the space to capture everything that goes on in this buzzing place.

When Andrew arrived at Bromley-by-Bow fifteen years ago there was nothing: a small church surrounded by some run-down buildings, a congregation of twelve eccentric elderly people, a salary for Andrew, and a church with £400 in the bank. He started by building relationships, giving one young woman, for instance, the keys to the building as a demonstration of trust. The congregation then agreed to offer their underused buildings to the community. Some artists living locally gave art classes in return for the use of the space rent free. Then came the Nursery Centre, the Pie in the Sky café, Community Education, the Bengali Outreach Project, the Toy Library, the Language Project, Vocational Training, the Community Care Project, Project Sinai and, most recently, the magnificent new building that houses the Health Centre. The latest list of projects, classes and initiatives runs to over one hundred and twenty-five activities a week. The centre as a whole had a gross revenue in 1998 of £2 million and employs over a hundred people. It has just signed a partnership agreement with a £200 million housing and regeneration company.

More is planned for the years ahead. The centre has redeveloped the park area around it, has developed supported housing locally for single elderly people, has bought the nearby site to extend its physical facilities, and turned an old burial site into a wildlife garden and adventure playground. The money comes from a wide range of partnerships including local businesses, health authorities, local authorities, central government, the European Union and charitable trusts. In 1995 the centre was awarded the BITC Dragon Award for Partnership by the City of London at their annual banquet but Andrew has now extended the partnership idea to Northern Ireland, forging links with the town of Enniskillen, in the belief that cross-cultural ideas apply to that part of the UK as much as they do to the East End of London. Building on his own experience he has launched a project to identify 2000 social entrepreneurs by the year 2000. 'They are bursting out of the woodwork. We just need to spot them and connect them together in what we are now calling the Community action Network.'

How did this milkman's son from Bradford come to find himself regenerating Bromley by Bow, perhaps even London itself and the rest of the land, by his example – all this in his early forties? It is an intriguing story, one that should give hope to many and which suggests that religious organizations still have an important part to play in our society if they can focus on where they are needed.

Andrew was one of twins, with an elder brother. His parents were hard-working Yorkshire folk, Baptist church-goers. His father believed that 'you just get on with life as it comes.' But Andrew was different, 'endlessly asking questions,' encouraged by his mother. School didn't satisfy his curiosity so he left at sixteen to start his work as a Post Office apprentice. Then he met John Shaw, the newly arrived minister at the local Baptist church. 'John introduced me to the "Why?" questions' and made religion interesting for the first time. Encouraged by John, Andrew applied to study at theological college, where he met another unusual and exciting cleric, Michael Taylor the Principal of the college. He needed A levels to get in. He got them in thirty weeks and married a few weeks before entering the college.

After four years there, Andrew was ready for a parish, but not for him the standard parish pattern. He had his next lucky break, going to work in Kingston with Eric Blakebrough, the visionary head of Kaleidoscope, the drug rehabilitation centre which was attached to his Kingston church. Eric was a strong role model. 'He connected theology with practicality and showed me how you could take nothing and turn it into something.' During his time there Andrew was largely responsible for organizing a National Campaign for Central America and led an investigative team there and to Washington – an interesting piece of alchemy which also boosted his self-confidence. Then came the offer of a traditional parish in Birmingham and the usual advice from well-meaning elders to establish himself before branching out. At the same time he was offered the opportunity to take on the challenge of a run-down church in London's East End. It was Bromley-by-Bow, at that time a forgotten nowhere part of Tower Hamlets.

Reason struggled with instinct, head with heart. Instinct won. He went to the East End. It has been hard work. Building relationships and partnerships is a never-ending task. Once built, they require maintenance and Andrew is a builder at heart. But there is now a large team to help him – all the staff members as well as a network of Council members, management committee members, volunteers, Friends of the Centre and many less formal supporters. Andrew has to some extent freed himself for other projects.

Curiosity; inspiring teachers, even though they came a little later for Andrew; a great role model and patron in Eric Blakebrough; an early success to prove to himself that he too could create something out of nothing; but, most of all, what inspired Andrew, was a burning need to connect theology with practicality, to show what can happen if you believe in people, offer them hope and give them the chance to turn that hope into practical action.

Joanne McFarlane

(Silk Scarves)

JOANNE McFARLANE IS NOT YET A name to conjure with for we caught her at the start of her business career, but if her life to date is any guide she will be hitting the headlines in the fashion textile world before too long. At present, with only her dog for company, she designs and makes silk and velvet scarves in the bedroom of her south London flat, selling them in Greenwich Market. Joanne is backed by a grant and loan from the Prince's Youth Business Trust, which has the best success record of any venture capital fund. Joanne is featured in this group of alchemists as an example of the many women who start their own small enterprises, preferring the challenges and risks of independence to jobs in organizations.

Joanne takes her designs from nature, often from the patterns of leaves that she finds in Kew Gardens or Greenwich Park, photographing or sketching them. She scans the images into her Apple computer and plays around with them on Photoshop, finally printing them out on to acetate, which she then silk-screens on to silk or by another process on to the velvets. In the second year of this venture she has an income of some £20,000 a year on which she says she can survive quite comfortably. 'Of course, there's always the worry – can you pay the bills, pay back the loans – but so far I've managed and the loans will be paid off next August.'

She oozes self-confidence: 'you've got to believe it will happen and then it will.' Where did she learn her computer skills? 'My dad was ill back in Oldham so I went to look after him for six weeks. I took all the manuals out of the library and read them. If I didn't understand them I got another book until I had it all worked out.'

'Did your father have a computer?'

'No'

'Did you?'

'No – but I memorized the procedures and when I got back to London and was able to buy one, I just put them to work.'

This from someone who left school with just two CSEs. But her experience at the school had helped to harden her resolve. She was the only black girl in the whole school and 'it was a horrible, horrible experience'. The staff publicly accused her of cheating when she came top in

English, many of the girls were pregnant before they left and she met no one who believed in her ability or talents. 'But I was determined that I was not going to be like the other girls.'

Joanne's father came from Jamaica on the *Windrush* and settled in Oldham where he got a job in the textile industry. Her mother followed soon after and worked as a machinist in the clothing industry – so textiles were in Joanne's past. The parents had high expectations of all their children. Joanne's eldest brother is an architect and the next eldest works for the Inland Revenue. Joanne was the third child and much was expected of her too. 'But there were six of us in this small house, including my younger sister with whom I shared a room. I had to get out. The library was my retreat. I went there every day and read everything I could get my hands on.' That is where she got her essential education.

Leaving school with a sigh of relief, Joanne applied to the local college to study fashion. They turned her down. She sharpened up her act and her portfolio, and tried again. This time she was accepted and so began what she thinks of as two great years. Asked by a local hotel to organize a fashion show for them, she took on the challenge even though the hotel offered nothing except the venue. She recruited twenty-two designers, took charge of the publicity, found models, sold advertising space and co-ordinated the show. It happened, made a little money *and* she sold all her own designs. She was nineteen and on her way.

Were there any key figures at her college? we asked her. 'Well, there was Mrs. Scott. She really pushed me and the more you gave the more she demanded. She was never satisfied. But a couple of years ago I returned to the college and asked if I could have back the portfolio of my last year's work that I had handed in but never seen again. "Oh Mrs Scott took it with her when she left. She wanted to use it as an example at her next school." So, finally, I knew that she approved. And no, I never did see it or her again.'

After the London College of Fashion she got a job right away, where she was thrown in at the deep end, doing menswear designs. She liked the work but she found herself, as a lone woman designer, ignored. 'They wouldn't even look at me when they spoke.' So she left, without a job to go to. '"Make scarves," my architect brother said and I was determined by then to start my own business, but I was too old to apply to the Prince's Youth Business Trust who had a cut-off age of twenty-five. Then by chance I overheard someone in the Post Office saying that they had raised the age to thirty. I checked it out and it was true. So I applied and they gave me a development loan to prove that I could make the scarves.'

She passed the test, researched and found the other loans and grants along with £40 per week from Greenwich Enterprise for the first six months, bought her computer, settled into her flat and found herself in business. That was two years ago. But the Prince's Trust do something else besides providing loans and grants. They give you a mentor. In Joanne's case it is Sue McDiarmid who has her own business in children's clothing. 'I see her on average once a month and she is a great help. Apart from general advice, she helps me to get in touch with buyers and deciding what to take them.' Although Joanna says that she isn't lonely, it is always encouraging to have an ally on call.

She has hopes and plans: from scarves to simple outfits; a design show; a shop in Covent Garden one day. But right now it is hard work, which only she can do. Away for a weekend at a trade exhibition, she asked a friend to sell her scarves for her at the market. 'She sold £200 worth which she was very pleased with, but I knew that I could have sold twice that number.' With her bubbly personality and self-confidence we could well believe it. As Joanne kept saying, 'You've got to believe it will happen.'

John McLaren

(Masterprize Composers' Competition)

IMAGINE YOURSELF AS A SUCCESSFUL BANKER in your early forties, but uncomfortable in your own skin, not too proud of what you do even though you do it well. Would you first, in your spare time, dream up, create and manage an international music competition and, later, use your summer holiday to write a novel, ignore 'gleeful' rejections by every agent, get it published and see it become a best-seller?

John McLaren did just that. Masterprize, an international competition for composers, was launched in 1996 and had its first final on 7 April 1998 at the Barbican. The London Symphony Orchestra, conducted by Daniel Harding, played the compositions of the six finalists. The concert was broadcast live on Radio 3 and on forty radio stations around the world. The jury for the final included Vladimir Ashkenazy and Thomas Hampson while Cherie Blair presented the prizes to the winners.

In the preceding months more than 1000 scores from sixty countries had been whittled down by an international panel to an eventual short-list of six, which were published on a CD by BBC *Music Magazine* and EMI and broadcast by twenty-six radio partners around the world. Their listeners voted for their choice of winner, with this worldwide listeners' choice ranking equal to that of the jury.

It was, and is, quite an undertaking. It wasn't John's business. He had enough to be getting on with in the rest of his life. He didn't come from a particularly musical or entrepreneurial family and he had never done anything like it before. He didn't do it alone, of course. The Masterprize partners are BBC Radio 3, EMI, the LSO, BBC *Music Magazine*, and BBC World Service, plus the network of radio stations around the world, but John had the idea, found and enthused the other partners and ran the small organizing group.

A music lover himself, 'I felt sad and puzzled that there is such a gap today between music lovers and composers' he wanted to find a way to allow new classical compositions to reach the general public and so devised a competition that not only awarded substantial cash prizes to the winners but also, as part of its process, offered their compositions to a broad international audience of music lovers.

It required imagination, self-confidence and a bit of cheek, quite a lot of determination and the ability to persuade others – all the ingredients of the successful alchemist. You also have to be extraordinarily well organized. You can sense that in his portrait. An immaculately tidy home, a carefully composed manner which conceals the controlled energy within, the three very different personae in one life. For, today, John McLaren is still a part-time banker and the director of four companies, but he is also the Chairman of Masterprize and a novelist, about to publish his third book. By any standards he is a man of parts.

The second child of a stable family (his father was an executive with British Steel), he saw school and university as part of an unavoidable obstacle course on the way to life, ending with an undistinguished degree in law. Few, then, would have predicted what he would have achieved before he was fifty. I doubt that he did himself. 'I didn't know what I wanted to be,' he says. He joined the Foreign Office, more to see the world than because he had a passion to be a diplomat. What he hadn't counted on was the skill in writing that he had to develop to produce his reports, one that was later to help him write his novel in double-quick time. Required to learn a language after joining, he volunteered to take Japanese, a tough two-year course in Sheffield and Japan, because he calculated that it would offer him the most options in his diplomatic future.

He loved the language and Japan, and did well, so well that Barings, the British merchant bank, lured him away from the Foreign Office on a long leave of absence to be their man in Japan, in which capacity he started a venture capital business for them. It was through that first decision and its consequences that John realized that you don't just have to go with the flow, that you can influence your own destiny and chart your own course in life if, of course, you know where you want to go. He had also discovered and enjoyed the 'I did that' feeling that you get from seeing the results of an initiative that you had started – one that is hard to find in a big organization.

That feeling was reinforced by his next move, to a venture capital business in San Francisco with Silicon Valley and its entrepreneurs down the road. 'I was fascinated to watch enterprises starting from nothing, two or three people getting together and saying "Let's do it".' Wooed back to London by Morgan Grenfell, at that time Britain's leading merchant bank, he was almost bound to be restless, even though he had big responsibilities as a director and some fascinating assignments. One thing, however, he had learnt in his banking career thus far was how to make compelling presentations to important people. He felt no awe of them and no nervousness. A capacity to persuade, even to charm, is a necessary ingredient in alchemy if anything is to come from a new idea.

Restlessness, even boredom, is a favourable breeding ground. John believes that creativity is part of the human condition. While many people put their creativity to work in their job or in their families, in their hobbies or their gardens, or even, sadly, in crime, for John the creative urge increasingly focused on his love of music and books. Creativity is not enough, of course. There has also to be a sort of dogged determination combined, in John's case, with the ability for some rigorous analysis: 'When people say it can't be done, I ask them why not and if I agree with them I give it up, but if they just mean it's difficult then I will find a way around it.'

Unlike most of our other alchemists, John has had no great mentors or searing experiences so far. From each of his careers he has drawn something, until his life looks like a planned learning experience, a seamless progression towards independence. But, apparently, he nearly died when an infant. Did his mother's special care for him thereafter give him more self-confidence? The family moved house five times in the course of his father's career. Did this mobility combined with the security of the family make him more at ease with switching careers and countries? At university he relied on a lecturer's hints of likely questions to skimp his preparation for the examinations and nearly failed. Did this jolt to his self-esteem make him more careful in his analysis of problems and in his assessment of people? Did his elder brother's sure vision and plan for his life ahead make John, the second son, more carefree, more of an explorer instead?

We cannot know. John, however, is convinced that we shall all have to be explorers of a sort in the future. Plans for life don't work nowadays – any more than his did.

Julia Middleton
(Common Purpose)

THE NEW ALCHEMISTS JULIA MIDDLETON

179

JULIA'S PORTRAIT SHOWS HER WITH HER five young children, her husband Rupert and a group from one of the local Common Purpose programmes. They are the three focal points of her existence, each one a priority. Others would find the complexity of her life daunting. For Julia the different elements interweave to support each other. Her successive pregnancies she calls 'sabbaticals', during which she thought up and came back to launch yet another venture. But a life wholly devoted to the family would be boring – 'for them as well as me' – and, without the wisdom, advice and calm presence of her husband, and the 'huge happiness' of their life together she might not have the emotional security that acts as the base for her risky ventures.

For example, Julia started Common Purpose in 1988. Her daughter Emma had just been born. She herself was about to return to her job at the Industrial Society. Rupert was away on a business course in America for four months. He returned to be confronted by the news that she had left her job, had decided, after hearing about the success of the Community Leadership Programmes in America, to start something similar in the UK and had already raised half a million pounds in sponsorship. Three months later she was pregnant again – another sabbatical, but rather shorter this time. There was work to be done.

Common Purpose runs a unique series of educational programmes for the rising generation of decision makers from all the different sectors of a town or city, private, public, voluntary and community. The programmes build bridges between the sectors, create networks, cross boundaries and broaden the horizons of those who will soon be responsible for large chunks of our lives. At their best they turn specialists into partners and invigorate our communities. The excitement of those who go on the courses is infectious.

After only ten years the programmes operate in over forty cities in the UK and have now started in Ireland, Sweden, Germany and Australia. It is a big operation with 120 paid staff, a turnover of more than £3 million and an advisory forum with some sixty of the most interesting people in Britain. How Julia came to be the force she is, the values she holds and the way she applies them, contains messages for many who dream of making the difference that she has done.

She tells how her father, a young man from an underprivileged background, was travelling on a train at the start of the last war. He heard two older men making what he thought were unpatriotic comments about the war so he made a citizen's arrest. One of the two turned out to be Charles Peat of Peat Marwick, the accountants. Surprised, impressed and contrite, Peat offered him a job, there and then. Julia believes that this story inspired her 'to say boo to a goose' and to be unterrified of anyone.

Julia also inherited her father's rebellious streak and quickly worked out that rebels are only productive if they are at the head of things. 'It takes a lot to manage rebels', she says today. 'I was one so I can.' Her mother too, she feels, only recently began to take charge of her own life, a mistake that Julia did not want to make.

The second child, with two brothers, Julia was fortunate in that her parents, by now living abroad, took her with them, even though they sent her two brothers to board at a public school. Instead, she went to the French Lycée, first in New York, then outside Geneva and later in London. There she met a more polyglot international bunch of people, learnt French and acquired republican sympathies. It was an exciting time, but 'I was an academic failure' she thought, until she went from the London Lycée to a local one in France, where she found herself at the top of the class. Unexpected success is a great boost to confidence so, when she was later told, back at the London Lycée, that she would never pass her baccalaureate it was just the trigger that the rebel needed. She passed and went on to study at the LSE.

It was later, at work, that she met some of the people who were to be models and mentors for her, John Garnett, Julia Cleverdon and Rupert Middleton, all at the Industrial Society and in their different ways, visionaries, leaders, good friends and counsellors. She was fortunate to find them all in one place at the same time. It was there that she had her first taste of successful alchemy – creating Head Start, a programme that provided school leavers in the inner cities with training and professional advice direct from their would-be employers. Within a couple of years she found herself leading a group of sixty people with programmes in twenty cities 'And they told me that I would never be a leader!'

One of Julia's secrets is her greediness to learn from others. In selecting her Chairmen for Common Purpose she has looked for people from whom she can glean something new. From a former boss she learnt that simple inefficiency, and the lack of attention to detail, is a great waste of time and energy. Another of her secrets is a positive approach to life: 'I can always find a good side to every situation.' She also believes that it is criminal to spend too much of your life worrying about things which don't really matter. This outlook on life is easier when you feel comfortable in your own skin, as Julia obviously does. There is no need then to look over your shoulder at what others think or how others do, to hanker after the honours and enticements of conventional society, or to seek to beat others at their game.

Meeting an old teacher one day in the street, he looked at her thoughtfully and said 'Julia, you look as if you haven't changed as much as you ought to have.' It was a compliment of sorts, she felt, as if he was implying that the rebellious streak was still there, that she hadn't conformed or settled down. Alchemists don't. They are always looking for new fields to explore, new ideas to develop, new projects to start. What Julia does next, if and when she feels it right to hand Common Purpose over to the next generation of leaders, is a question that intrigues many, including, one suspects, herself.

Geoff Mulgan

(Demos Think Tank)

IN GEOFF MULGAN'S HOME YOU ARE as likely to find a work group discussing a social issue as to discover him cooking one of his gourmet meals, that is when he is not writing a paper or pamphlet, many of them stacked beside his chair in the portrait.

In 1993 Geoff Mulgan created Demos, 'an independent think tank committed to radical thinking on the long-term problems facing the UK and other advanced industrial societies'. He had no money of his own and no backers. Eventually one individual donated £5000, which paid for three months' rent – and a launch party. He was thirty years old. In the few years since that party Demos has sprayed the country with a heady mixture of pamphlets, seminars, conferences and books, some more way out than others but all challenging the *status quo* and advocating new ways of thinking about society in all its aspects.

Geoff left Demos in 1997 to take up a role in the centre of government, attracted by the opportunity to turn ideas into reality, but it is his creation of Demos that earns him a place in this book. 'I like creating institutions,' he says, as do most of our alchemists, and he has been involved in conceiving and launching institutions as varied as Red Wedge, the University for Industry and more recently the Social Exclusion Unit, but it requires a certain presumption to found one designed to help shape the politics of the next century when one is still in one's twenties. Perhaps that is the time to do it, before the bright gleams of new ideas become clouded by the practicalities of power and increasing responsibilities. If so, then Geoff's alchemy needs to be imitated by others. He himself is impressed by the young talent now in the Demos he left behind, many of whom are even younger than he was at the beginning.

In Geoff Mulgan's case the seeds of social alchemy were visible early on. At the age of fourteen, he was recruiting teenagers for the trades unions, leading them in campaigns against the National Front, knocking on doors, marching, fund raising. He was, he says, always questioning, reading voraciously, mixing adolescent rebellion with idealism, forever in trouble with authority. 'It was the hypocrisy I hated, the gap between the official values of society and what it does.' It must have left his parents 'slightly bemused' he says but they remained loving and supportive. He was, after all, the third child who is traditionally more indulged. And he was clever, winning a scholarship to a public school and going on to Oxford in due course where, again, he was more concerned with Town than Gown, recruiting the unemployed into trades unions, for example, and still organizing action against the National Front. Always it was practical action that appealed, not political parties or ideas.

Then it was straight from Oxford to the GLC of Ken Livingstone, arriving there nine days before its abolition was announced. There he learnt that it is not enough to be open to new ideas, as that organization famously was. Because the GLC was also badly mismanaged and politically self-indulgent it was ineffective and ultimately doomed. Redundant at its closure, he applied for and won a Harkness Fellowship which brought him to study at MIT where the computer buffs were reinventing the world. He also got to work for the Democrats at the Iowa Primary in 1987, with the likes of Al Gore, Michael Dukakis and Jesse Jackson. He went to America with many adverse stereotypes in his mind, most of which, he says, were quickly disproved. America with its energy, its belief in the future and in the vitality of its institutions left its mark.

Geoff came back to live a portfolio life, a mix of consultancy, academic and radio work, plus a lot of social action: Red Wedge, for instance, a campaigning organization of pop musicians, comedians and artists who toured the country prodding the social awareness of the young, putting on concerts in the evenings and meetings with local politicians in the daytime – 'fascinating dialogues of the deaf'. Then, alchemy stirring again, he put together a consortium of pirate radio stations and bankers to bid for a radio licence for London. It failed, twice. But Geoff learnt that as well as content and money you also have to lobby the decision makers.

But he remains, he insists, a semi-civil servant at heart – 'I always wanted to work in government' – so when he was offered a high-paying job as a Eurocrat in Brussels he accepted, only to be rung by Gordon Brown a week before he left saying, 'Come and run my office.' 'It was one of those events that change one's life. Had that call come one week

187

later mine might have been very different.' Gordon Brown was fascinating to work for, although very demanding. 'I've never come across such a mental capacity for strategic thinking.' Besides the insight that the experience gave him into the intricacies of political strategy, he met the leaders of the then Labour Party, connections which were later to prove very useful.

But Labour lost the 1992 election, and the thought of five more years of drafting speeches and position papers in opposition did not appeal. Geoff left, not at all clear what he wanted to do. For all his piercing analytical intelligence, he is an opportunist in his own life, refusing to plan ahead in any detail. 'I set up Demos for want of anything else to do,' he says. Not quite true, because it grew out of a discussion group involving Martin Jacques, late editor of *Marxism Today,* among others, where the idea of a think tank was mooted. 'But like all such ideas, it needs someone to pick it up and give their life to it for a bit.' It was scary, not financially because they never borrowed any money, but because of the loss of credibility if it failed; and it was very hard work for a while, with a staff of two to produce all the papers as well as licking the envelopes, searching for funding and answering the telephone. 'These things are fun if its your own baby and anyway I was used to it.'

Given that his parents were conventional middle-class professionals, a music publisher and a teacher, where did all this radical social alchemy come from? Geoff tells an intriguing story: 'I looked up the name "Mulgan" on the Internet the other day. It's an unusual name, being a corruption of Mulligan, so all the references were to me or my distant cousins in New Zealand whom I have never met. Every single one was concerned with social or political action. So maybe it's in my genes.' But there were other influences in his early life – an unlikely duo, for instance, the Liverpool docker who cleaned for his parents and a German Buddhist monk in Sri Lanka.

The docker he encountered when in his teens. 'He was about the most intelligent and perceptive person I had met, but a failure. He showed me what society looked like from the bottom up.' Then, aged seventeen, he spent a gap year before university in India, including three months in a Buddhist monastery in Sri Lanka, where he came across the German, an old man who had been a student of Jung and lived in a hut in the jungle. There the two of them talked out the old dilemma: 'Do you change yourself or society?' Add to these two mentors someone like Gordon Brown and you can sense some of the influences on Geoff's life. He was fortunate, you might say, but he made his own luck, thrusting himself into the fray at such an early age, driven not by personal ambition but by a passion to improve society and remove some of that hypocrisy which so annoyed him in his teens. Next step? A 'Do Tank' he surmises, but with Geoff Mulgan you never know where an opportunity for social alchemy will come from.

Julian Richer

(Entrepreneur)

193

ENERGY, PASSION AND INSTANT FRIENDLINESS ARE the first things you notice about Julian Richer. He moves fast, thinks fast and talks very fast. For a small man he fills a big space, even one as large as his seventy-foot-long penthouse apartment in the centre of London, portrayed here. He likes living well but that, it is clear, is not the point of his life. He is in a hurry and hungry for more chances to 'make a difference and add value'. Starting new things seems to be his passion and he is good at it. It is also the secret of his success – new ideas being the food he feeds off, particularly if they come from his own employees.

Not yet forty, he owns or presides over twenty businesses, most of which he has started himself. He aims to make that at least thirty before long, chief among them being his flagship company, Richer Sounds, the largest retailer of hi-fi equipment in the UK which he started from scratch when he was nineteen. It is now a £60 million wholly owned company with, he is proud to point out, an entry in the *Guinness Book of Records* six years running for more sales per square foot in its stores than any other retailer in the world.

Not content with that, Julian runs a small consultancy business, injecting his original, even wacky, ideas into other organizations. He has written two books about those ideas, demonstrated them on video and expounded them on conference platforms. The table in his office, for instance, is chest high, forcing all meetings to take place standing up. The mirror which says 'you are looking at the most important person in this shop' and the bell that customers are asked to ring if they feel well served, may seem gimmicky to some but they work, as do the free umbrellas given to those who buy a hi-fi when it's raining.

Less noticed, deliberately, than his businesses is the third of his time that he gives to charitable causes, and the five per cent of profits of his business that go into his charitable foundation. This foundation funds the requirements of nineteen GRPs – Generic Research Groups, two to five people drawn from his companies who take time out from work to investigate and do something about an array of social problems, which they themselves identify. A typical project is On the Right Track, terminals for homeless people and runaway kids which can be found at London railway stations and other locations. Each month Julian meets with the leaders of these project groups, and believes that the work they do adds an important dimension to their lives. It must also, one suspects, add to the general culture of creativity in the businesses themselves.

He is fortunate, he points out, in having had many years of experience, including a few bad ones, but can still call himself young. That is because he started unusually early, beginning to trade aged only fourteen at his school, using his term's pocket money of £10 to buy a hi-fi unit from *Exchange and Mart* and selling it for £22. By the time he left school he had three helpers working for him on commission and, by spending half his earnings and saving half, he was left with £2000. He had discovered an early truth: that you can make more money more quickly by selling your expertise and turning it into a product than by selling your time. It is the clue to most entrepreneurial success, one that those who live on salaries and wages never discover.

Then he had some luck. He went to rent his first shop and the landlord not only let him have it without any premium but gave him a £20,000 loan to start the business in return for seventy-four per cent of the equity. Luck like that is, perhaps, earned rather than chanced upon. Something in the young man and his passion must have moved the older man to take a chance with him. Vic Odden, the landlord, did well out of the deal. The loan was repaid in nine months and the shares sold back to Julian over seven years for many times their initial value, but Julian credits Vic with giving him a great start and for his support over the following years with their mixture of success and failure.

At the end of his first full year of trading, for example, with a profit of £20,000, a sports car and a flashy flat, he was on top of the world. Next year this had changed into a loss of £130,000 which it took two years of struggle to turn around. He was twenty-one. It happened again six years later when he went from four to eighteen shops in one bound and had to retrench. This time he learnt and resolved not to overreach himself again. Successful alchemists learn from failures. The difference is that they remain undeterred when most of us would give up. Their passion keeps them going.

He was also 'lucky' to be introduced to Archie Norman who had just become Chairman of the failing Asda supermarket group. Norman

195

came to dinner and spent the evening scribbling, recording all Julian's imaginative ideas, many of which he was to introduce to Asda in the months to come. At the end of the meal he asked Julian to come and talk to his Board and later hired him as his personal consultant, throwing him into the stores and drawing out his impressions and ideas. Julian counts Archie Norman as one of the key influences in his life. This experience taught him that big organizations are really small ones with more noughts and made him realize that what he saw as common sense was not all that common. It was another boost to his self-confidence. The first book followed soon after.

Julian was not intellectually successful at school; surprisingly, perhaps, because his father had been a Fulbright Scholar at Harvard and was 'very clever'. But intellectual brilliance does not always make for success in life. His parent was independently-minded but not so good at business. 'I was very fond of my father, but he was perhaps too clever to be an entrepreneur. He could always see the down side where I saw the opportunities.' His mother started a clothes shop and so, maybe because of that, 'retailing was always in my blood,' says Julian. But perhaps because he was also small in stature, he needed to be more pushy and unconventional than most first-borns usually are. Embarrassed, too, by the problems caused by his parents' relative poverty, he wanted for himself the freedom that money brings. Add to these spurs a socially aware housemaster at his public school who brought out the social conscience in Julian and you can see some of the key influences in his life.

In an unexpected and unusual way, school was a springboard to life in the outside world, confirming him as a successful businessman in the making. With his burgeoning self-confidence further reinforced by Vic Odden and Archie Norman he was ready made for entrepreneurship. There is also Rosie, sitting by him in the portrait, who added stability to his restlessness. They met when he was twenty-one and have been together ever since. Rosie is in many ways his opposite – a country lover, horsewoman, art collector and model. She is the perfect counterpart to his restless alchemy and, in their Yorkshire home, structures the pauses in his busyness that are, perhaps, the well-spring of his creativity and passions.

Julian Richer said that his purpose in life was to make a difference and add value. His record of constructive alchemy in business, ideas and social action is already outstanding. Few can doubt that there is more to come. 'If I was on a beach in the South of France I would be bored out of my mind. I feel that I am at an interesting crossroads in my life and would like to take on a much bigger challenge.'

Dennis Stevenson

(Company Chairman and the New Tate)

DENNIS STEVENSON SEEMED DESTINED IN HIS youth to become a distinguished academic in a great university But there was an unexpected hitch. Instead of the First Class Honours that everyone confidently expected he got a lower Second. The set-back stunned him, but set him free to begin to be what he is today, a radical chairman of great institutions, both private and public, a provoker, goad and stimulus to the powerful behind the scenes and one of the more unusual and exceptional figures of our times.

He is a different sort of alchemist from most of our other examples in that he chooses to work through great organizations in order to 'make something out of nothing or to turn base metal into gold'. Organizations add leverage to his imagination and to his constant endeavour to do what he can to make the world a bit better – for everyone. Distinctly left-wing in his youth, he has never lost his radical reforming urge, but has chosen to do what he does outside formal politics.

He is pictured standing in front of what was the Bankside Power Station as it begins its transformation into the new Tate Gallery of Modern Art. As Chairman of the Trustees of the Tate from 1989 until 1998, it was his and Nicholas Serota's vision and energy that first saw the potential of this wasted building, then found the support and the funds to turn it into the cultural centre that it will become, although Nicholas Serota and his team at the Tate have the challenge of making the dream become hard reality. The new Tate is also a signal example of his consistent principle of maintaining a balance in his life between business and social enterprises. Alchemy is needed in both arenas, and Dennis early on realized that the benefits that commercial enterprise can confer are not limited to the shareholders. 'A man who sets up a business in Hartlepool and employs forty people probably does more good than a social worker.'

In the portrait he is looking across at St Paul's Cathedral and the City, representing the business side of his life, and can be seen striding off the end of the picture to another engagement. He is a busy alchemist, injecting his imagination, passion and energy into the Boards of some sixteen organizations, private and public. It is Dennis's great ability to conceive of what might be and then to work with and through his chief executives and their people to make it happen. 'I never have an office or a secretary in any organization where I am Chairman. I perch where I can and the chief executive's secretary opens everything, and I mean everything, addressed to me.' That way there are complete trust and no secrets. As a result he can be chairman of two huge corporations, Pearson, the publishing and media group, and Aertic Group PLC, one of the largest aircraft businesses in the world – both of which he is transforming, as well as being, until July 1998, Chairman of the Trustees of the Tate. 'I thrive on stimulating and interesting projects,' he says. 'As long as they help to improve people's lives in some way.'

Dennis's parents gave him a good Scottish beginning in a stable home. Unlike most of our alchemists he was the eldest child. His father's family had always been ministers in the Church of Scotland or decent professional people. His mother was largely self-taught although clever and determined enough to win a scholarship to Cambridge in the days when women were a rarity there. The sense of principle, the brains and the determination obviously resurfaced in Dennis, helped by two great teachers at his school but, after the early shock of that missed First and the realization that life was not necessarily going to unroll effortlessly before him as it had so far, he took a firm control of his own destiny.

He was also skilled at exploiting his luck. 'Entrepreneurs are not born,' he insists. 'They happen.' Early in his career, at the time of the Heath government, he publicly criticized a draconian bill going through Parliament seeking to regulate pop festivals, which would almost legislate them out of existence. As a result Peter Walker, the Minister concerned, asked him to draft a code of practice for pop festivals and gave him, aged twenty-five, a small team of civil servants to help. His code is still the guidebook for all pop festivals. So began his habit of splitting his time between private business and public service.

It was to continue when Peter Walker then asked him to become Chairman of the ambitious New Town project at Peterlee in the northeast. It was an extraordinary act of faith on his part. Stevenson was twenty-six, known to be left-wing, and he was to chair a Tory quango responsible for 2000 people and several hundred million pounds in a depressed mining area. It was also a courageous decision by Dennis, if rather contrary to his view that entrepreneurs don't take risks if they can help it. But the challenge was irresistible, even though it had to be combined with running his company back in London and starting a family. 'If I had not had my own business I couldn't have done it.' He did the job for ten years and after some initial local hostility this imported whiz-kid won the hearts of the local people.

In many ways he feels that successful creation of the Aycliffe and Peterlee New Town Development Corporation is the best thing he has done. If anything was an example of making something out of nothing this was it and it gave Dennis a taste, and a reputation, for major public service projects. More was to follow over the years, some in the public eye, some more discreet. Alchemists rarely receive the endorsement of the Establishment, but Lord Stevenson CBE, as he is now at the age of fifty-three, has always been adept at winning the enthusiasm of the powerful for his imaginative ideas. The successful alchemist's ability to persuade, even to charm, is his in large measure. Yet for all his enthusiasm for change and improvement he is obviously sincere when he says, 'The most exciting things in my life are my wife and children.' One feels that without the solid base of his family, and the space he is careful to give them in his crowded life, he might have lost his way in a bundle of enthusiasms.

Few have all Dennis Stevenson's talents, but we have to admire the way he rebounded from what seemed, at the end of his college career, a major set-back. He may call what followed 'luck', but he prepared the ground for it, both by not being shy to speak his mind on issues that personally concerned him and by building a network of potentially useful contacts. He then had the courage to take on the challenges which were the consequences of his outspokenness. These habits continue. He would say that his Chairmanship of the Tate, possibly also of Pearson, came about because he spoke his mind and ended up being asked to take on the responsibility for the institution. It is the mixture of concern for the general good, integrity and organizing skills that has made him such an influential figure in a wide variety of arenas.

Jane Tewson

(Comic Relief and Pilotlight)

206

IN THE BARN THAT SHE LIVES in, behind the house where she grew up, with her husband and children in the background, Jane Tewson dreams of changing the world. She sees a world where too many are excluded from societies that measure everything in money, where too many people have no voice, no recognition of what they can do, no way of contributing to the communities in which they live. So two years ago she started Pilotlight to do something about it. It was, she says, the natural successor to Charity Projects which she began back in 1984, the charity that gave birth to Comic Relief and Red Nose, and in the process revolutionized fund raising and our view of charities. So far, Comic Relief has raised £166 million for its causes and three out of four of us have been involved in some part of Red Nose fun.

Pilotlight is tiny, just Jane and three part-timers, and will stay tiny, but from its London base it hopes to act as a catalyst for a movement that will infect the minds of people everywhere – a social revolution, she calls it. A pilot light is a small burner kept alight to light another and Jane sees her creation as the centre of an expanding network of initiatives, which will give a voice to all outsiders. It will allow the excluded not only to influence their world but to contribute to it. 'When I see the world through the eyes of some of the homeless I get terribly passionate and excited about what we are doing. I am a maverick voice that can say what people don't want to hear. I can dare to challenge the government. What do they really mean, I ask them, by "The Giving Age", which is a terribly patronizing phrase?'

It is early days yet but already Pilotlight has initiated several imaginative projects. One, Real Deal, has brought a hundred young disadvantaged youths together to tell those in power of their views and experiences – to give them a voice at party conferences, in Downing Street, at local seminars and meetings. Real Deal, Jane says, gives the *real* experts a chance to make positive change. Going international, a further project is helping the livestock-herding Maasai people of Kenya to make their voice heard as they see their traditional lands appropriated. A third is aimed at raising our awareness of the plight of refugees and asylum seekers, who are another voiceless community. In all these projects Pilotlight is the catalyst, bringing together an alliance of organizations from business, government and the voluntary sector.

But the big one is yet to start. ONE20 it is called, from the idea that everyone should give one twentieth of their time or 120 minutes a week, to their community. Giving time not money enfranchises everyone, not just the rich, because, Jane believes passionately that everyone has something to contribute if we can only find the right channel. Such an idea could reinvigorate our communities were it to happen, giving meaning to life and changing our view of human nature, because contributing as opposed to receiving brings out the best in people. Jane wants to change the image and the language of what has been called volunteering so that the contribution of time becomes as much a part of our culture as our annual holidays, our entitlement and our pleasure, as well as our opportunity to discover that we as individuals can exert real, tangible influence, that we can change a part of our world.

Aged nineteen, Jane had already discovered 'that anything is possible' and she has never looked back. She failed all her A level examinations, she was dyslexic and, in spite of a good local school, was not at her best in written exams. Undaunted, she went off to nearby Oxford to have some extra tuition and earned her keep as a cleaner. Cheekily, she also sneaked her way into those university lectures that took her fancy. No one checked and no one stopped her. She probably learnt more, she says, than those who were compelled to go. She also made lots of friends and contacts and began to appreciate 'That it was OK to be different'.

Already interested in the plight of disadvantaged people she became a project co-ordinator at Mencap but walked out one day in anger and frustration at their refusal to let tpeople with learning disabilities speak for themselves. The next week she started Charity Projects with the aim of giving a voice to the disadvantaged. 'I had heard of the Saatchi brothers so I went along and sat in their office hoping to see them and to ask them for a donation to start my idea. I didn't see them in the end but I was allowed in to see Tim Bell. He listened and gave me four years' wages, £40,000, and told me to go off and get started. I had never met him before.'

Charity Projects set out to put the fun into fund raising. 'We also wanted to make it clear that just because people used four-letter words it didn't mean that they couldn't be compassionate.' But they imposed certain conditions on those to whom they then gave the money they raised. No money, for example, to any organization working with people with learning disabilities, that does not give a place on their Board to some of those they were designed to help. 'They didn't like that one little bit but we had the money so they had to agree.' That came about after Jane had been to Africa, and quickly realized that the disadvantaged there needed both sustained support and to be able to tell their story themselves. Hence the idea of Comic Relief and the combination of comedy, documentaries and charity projects. Richard Curtis, the screen writer, organized the comedy and the broadcasts; Jane dealt with the project end. It has been, of course, a huge and well-publicized success story which continues, but now without Jane. 'I was very proud of Charity Projects but I could see new situations arriving, refugees, the homeless and so on. They needed a new organization. So I started it.'

She was also, however, involved in the very personal project of starting a family which has meant a lot of juggling with time and responsibilities. But Jane is resilient although, she says, very tired at times. Aged forty-one, she has only one regret: that she never went to university properly. 'I need to go back and get a degree just to prove that I can do it.' Prove it to herself, presumably, because no one else would doubt that she could do anything she set her mind to. As she herself says, 'With my beliefs you can go anywhere at any time and people will let you in.'

She has, she says, been very lucky. Lucky in her parents, two very liberal-minded doctors, who gave her, two older sisters and a younger brother a wonderful childhood. 'My mother was very sparky. There's a wild streak in her.' Lucky, she says, in the people she has met since then, although you get the sense that she makes sure she meets them. 'I don't socialize. Life's too short for nice conversations. But if you share emotional experiences with someone, visiting homeless people in Soho for instance, you make a real connection. And I'm good on committees, I think. I come in completely off-beam on a subject and people value that.'

She admits to few set-backs. Dyslexia, however, was a major one early on. She had problems at her first, private, school. Aged eleven, she wrote 'bollocks' in an essay instead of 'rowlocks' and was made to write out the correct word a hundred times. Her horrified parents took her away at once. The local comprehensive that she then went to was a genuinely creative place, which ignored her dyslexia, loved what she said and built her self-confidence. Since then, confidence and courage have never been her problem. As for the future: 'My heart's still popping out all over the place.'

Tim Waterstone

(Waterstone's bookstores)

PICTURED HERE IN HIS NEW HOUSE with his wife Rosie and their two small daughters, sitting with a pile of his own novels by his side, there is little to indicate that Tim Waterstone was the man who revolutionized bookselling in Britain and who is now Chairman of the largest chain of bookstores in Europe – the HMV Media Group plc, which is the merger of Dillons, Waterstones and HMV. Yet Tim Waterstone's story could stand as a prototype of business alchemy, with all its excitements, problems, ups and downs.

There was not much in his early life to suggest what might lie ahead. The third child of a 'simple' family, he had a very conventional childhood – for those days. Much younger than his elder siblings, with a father away in the war in his early years, he became very close to his mother. After the war his father returned to his job as a tea planter and Tim was sent to a variety of small boarding-schools, then to public school and, eventually, to Cambridge. Not everyone would have relished such a traditional boarding-school education but Tim was unfazed by it. 'I enjoyed my schooldays. I was *quite* good at everything. And Cambridge was enormous fun.'

Life continued in a conventional way. He married his childhood sweetheart and started working for organizations, first in Calcutta but then, more significantly, for Allied Breweries where he stayed for nine years, mostly as a marketing manager. It was a good start to his career and he prospered. But then he moved to W H Smith who eventually sacked him after eight unhappy and frustrating years – 'I thought that I could do things so very much better than they were doing.'

For a man who now says, 'I don't particularly enjoy other people's businesses,' twenty years of your life seems a long time to spend in them. 'I needed the money' he says. Having divorced his first wife, married again and acquiring, by then, six children, he had school bills to pay and a growing family to support. But the experience wasn't all wasted. He discovered that he had a talent for marketing and he worked with Sir Derrick Holden-Brown, then the head of Allied Breweries, who was 'a great influence on my life; very entrepreneurial and imaginative. I admired his friendliness, the way he treated his people and the way he ran the company.' They still meet. Sir Derrick spotted Waterstone's entrepreneurial instincts almost before he did himself and told him recently, 'I thought it would always break out in the end.'

'The act of firing me was great. It released me to do my own thing, which is what I had always wanted to do.' And this time he knew what that was: to start a chain of bookstores with a radically new philosophy – huge stocks, late opening (Hatchards at that time closed at noon on Saturdays) as well as knowledgeable and friendly staff. There was no market research. 'It was so much what I wanted to do that I could not believe that it wouldn't work.' He had £6000 of his own, a loan of £10,000 from his father-in-law and some bank borrowing. 'It was ludicrous to think that I could build a national chain of bookstores starting with that. But I was determined to do it, absolutely determined. I stopped worrying about money and just said "I'm going to do this."'

The original shop opened in Old Brompton Road and failed to meet its first year's sales budget. But by then Tim knew he was on to the right thing. Private investors joined. Booksellers were supportive and 'every time we got any money we opened another store.' It was hard work, although it didn't feel like work. 'I couldn't keep out of the bookstores. I think that it was a major factor in the break-up of my second marriage.' It was also scary. 'I was terrified about meeting the payroll, and there were three times when I very nearly didn't; but the staff were wonderful, and they all had shares so they shared the worries.' There were, he says, two secrets to his success, apart from the introduction of the new way of selling books: 'It was the least centralized of all the chains; the local store manager took all his or her own decisions; and I had the trust of the publishers, they gave me extremely good credit terms and we always paid them on the due date, never late.'

Waterstone's became a great success. But then he sold it to W H Smith. 'I was in the middle of a personal recession, having got divorced again, and the country was heading for a major recession. I didn't want to see all that I had built collapse.' Why then buy it back some ten years later? 'I wasn't after Waterstone's. It was W H Smith that I was interested in, although Waterstones' was part of it. I felt that Smiths were destroying the middle ground of bookselling and I wanted to save it. I was astonished when their defence was to spin off Waterstone's. EMI, who owned Dillons, was interested in Waterstone's so we got together and made a joint bid.'

In retrospect it was obviously the right thing to do. 'It's wonderfully happy for me,' he says, 'and the staff are delighted; they feel safe at last. It's a fabulously happy part of my life.'

Tim used the interval between the two Waterstone's phases to launch a new business, a chain of stores for young children, Daisy and Tom. He was also starting a new family and writing his first novel. Was it, maybe, his fascination with books that fed his passion for Waterstone's? 'A good question,' he says. 'I love books and I love writing stories but no, it could have been anything; it was the marketing angle that really interested me, although I'm very happy that it turned out to be books. I also like swimming against the tide. I don't trust the received wisdom and want to prove it wrong. Entrepreneurial life is exhilarating if you have the right mind-set. I'm not a gambler. Entrepreneurs are often very conservative and prefer to take risks with other people's money. With banks like Warburg behind you, as in that last bid, it doesn't feel that risky.'

But entrepreneurs need to have a good deal of self-belief to fuel all that effort. 'I have developed a lot of self-confidence over the years,' Waterstone says. 'I think that it may even come across as arrogance at times. But I know that I can persuade people to go with me and that's a very important quality in life.' There was another thing: he grew up with a bit of a social chip on his shoulder. 'I hated the way people patronized my father, who was a good man but not rich, not conventionally successful. He had a Newcastle accent to the end of his life. I had a burning desire to make my name and yes, my parents would have been delighted at the way things have turned out.'

For a man with his ambition it must be satisfying to see that name writ large on so many high streets in Britain – 'and over the whole world before I end,' adds Tim Waterstone.

Stephen Woodhams

(Woodhams – Landscape Designs)

PLANTS AND PLOTTING, GARDEN PLOTTING THAT is, are at the centre of Stephen Woodhams' life and business. Seen here on his self-designed roof-top terrace, Stephen is about to dash off to a meeting with one of his clients. He has turned his passion into a successful business. The only thing that the photograph can't show is Stephen's love of food and cooking. His ultra-modern kitchen is two floors below in his stylish contemporary home off the Portobello Road in London.

Now he is thirty-four years old, and the business that he started ten years ago on his own has a turnover in excess of £1 million and twenty-six employees. It has four divisions which, he believes, all share his hallmark and feed off each other. The truth probably is that each represents one side of Stephen's interests and therefore they all reflect his ideas and personality.

Woodhams is first of all a flower shop, situated at No.1 Aldwych, London's newest hotel. Second, it is a landscape design business with a 5500 square foot warehouse. Third, Woodhams designs and executes 'floral events', occasions such as grand parties and weddings, even, recently, the floral setting for a fashion display in New York. Fourth, Stephen produces a range of merchandise such as containers or, indeed, watering cans, which reflect his own rather architectural approach to design. There is also a growing range of Stephen's books that help to publicize, explain and illustrate his approach, which he would say was a mix of the contemporary and the comfortable.

Stephen is busy. He delegates a lot of the work but for him it is important to put his own personal touch to everything if he can. He can be seen at Covent Garden's floral market most mornings at 4 a.m. 'People want my involvement, so I don't want it to get too much bigger in case I lose the chance to build relationships. I have clients who I first met when I designed their garden, then I did their daughter's wedding, now its her garden and maybe the christening of her child. I like that'.

'I was meant to do this. My grandfather was a nurseryman in Canterbury, growing roses and carnations for Moyses Stevens. I never met him, sadly, and I only discovered that he sold flowers to Moyses Stevens when I was a buyer there in my first job. It's nice that the world comes full circle.' He goes on to tell how his mother taught flower arranging in her spare time. He grew up surrounded by flowers and flower arranging. 'She says now that I'm doing all the things she wanted to do. She teases me about the way I do things. We never make a wired wedding bouquet as she used to do. Ours are always loose and hand-held.'

It was she who took him to Farnborough market as a schoolboy where he met George Ecclestone. George gave him work helping him to set up the flower stall he ran. It was George who told him, 'I wish I had discovered horticulture when I was your age' and it was with his earnings from George that he paid for the greenhouse he put up in the garden from which he sold tomatoes, cucumbers and bedding plants to his teachers at his secondary school. Stephen's business career had started early.

The younger, by nine years, of two children, 'I had a brilliant upbringing.' His father was a civil servant. 'He has a wonderfully focused mind and is great with numbers. I'm no good with numbers. I leave all that to my accountant but maybe a bit of my father's focusing has rubbed off on me.' Certainly his mother's love of both flowers and cooking has stayed with him. Naughty at primary school where he was almost expelled, he only started to work when he got to senior school and subconsciously realized, he now thinks, that he would need to learn if he wanted to succeed. The teachers weren't just the customers for the produce of his greenhouse, they clearly built his self-esteem and he can still reel off their names and their subjects.

Then it was off to train at Wisley, the gardens of the Royal Horticultural Society. 'Those were the best two years of my life so far. We were paid £40 per week and there were just twenty of us.' It was a steep learning curve with some wonderful gardeners, such as 'Harry Baker who could identify any apple that you handed him although we grew 400 different varieties'. Two years followed with an interior landscaping company and then, aged twenty-three, it was time to put his own name on his own business. He raised £5000 from one investor and got started, with £40 a week from the government's Youth Enterprise Scheme.

Why? 'Well, it wasn't for money, that's for sure. You don't go into horticulture if it's money you want.' There are many, he admits, who are after a steady job with a steady income, but not he. 'The world is too exciting. It is wonderful to be rewarded directly for something you have

223

done. I would like to leave my mark somewhere. I never felt that my father got the accolade for all the things he did in his job in the civil service.' Putting your name on your business is one way of leaving your mark. Yes, he agrees, and it's also a form of guarantee to your clients that you will stand by your work.

What he loves, he says, is the joy of working with flowers and 'making a lot of people happy' by what he does. 'I still don't feel I'm working.' Then there is his responsibility for his fellow workers. 'I've got this chap, he's been with me for six years, and I've watched him get married and start a family. It's wonderful to think that I have helped to make that possible for him. I used to get upset when any of my staff left me to set up on their own, but now I feel proud that I helped to give them that chance. . . . We are all creative. It is my job to try to draw it out from those who work with me.'

But how does he maintain his own creativity? 'Everywhere I go I collect images in my mind. For instance, in this club in New York I went to the lavatory and I realized that I could see right through the glass door, which was going to be a bit uncomfortable. But when I went inside and turned the lock the door became opaque. There was an electric current, apparently, which made the glass opaque when it was turned on. Later, back in London, I remembered that door when I needed one like it. I contacted the club, asked for the name of the German manufacturer and was able to get what I wanted to use in a garden.'

He has made his mark already. How would he advise those setting out in life? 'Be honest with yourself. Follow your heart.' So where is his own heart leading? 'I want to travel. I always envied the boys at school who had travelled so much more than I had. My parents only started travelling when they retired. I look at my clients who seem to be always on the move or living in three countries. I understand myself so much better when I'm abroad and come back invigorated.'

Meantime there is a new house to find, so that he can design its kitchen, its interior and its terrace garden in his unique Woodhams way. Stephen has made his own life and intends to go on that way, putting his mark on his world.

Michael Young
(School for Social Entrepreneurs, et al.)

MICHAEL YOUNG IS A PRINCE AMONG alchemists. Now aged eighty-three he has, at the last count, created forty-nine charities. The Open University was his idea, as was the Consumers' Association and their magazine *Which?*. Most recently he has launched the School for Social Entrepreneurs, hoping to encourage in others what has been his lifelong passion – launching new organizations to remedy some deficiency in society. He is pictured here at the heart of his institutional home and the birthplace of so many of his organizations, in Victoria Park Square in Bethnal Green. He can be seen, up a ladder, with the book *Young at Eighty,* which was written for his eightieth birthday by his associates and colleagues down the years, a tribute to Michael's life and work. Then, on the left, he is seen going to yet another initiative, passing underneath one of his own paintings.

Tony Flower, who has worked for many years with Michael, has described what one might call the Michael Young process of institutional creation: 'You spot a problem, imagine a solution and give it a working title. Then you write to everyone who might conceivably have an interest in it and many who don't; produce a paper taking in the resulting comments without once losing sight of the original notion; form a steering committee; set up a charitable trust; meet someone by chance on a train and invite him or her to become the unpaid director of the new organization; launch the new body at a press conference; couple this with an article in the *Guardian*; carpet-bomb the charitable foundations with grant applications; stick with the fledgeling organization for precisely as long as necessary and then push it out of the nest to make room for the other six organizations you are waiting to hatch that week.'

Michael has written fifteen books, most notably *Family and Kinship in East London,* which established his reputation as a sociologist with his feet in reality, and *The Rise of the Meritocracy,* which introduced a new word to the language. There were also numerous articles and papers, including, aged twenty-three in 1938, one on *Manpower Planning in the War* which became the basis of government policy for the next six years. He was the principal author of the manifesto for the Labour Party in the 1945 election, the first lecturer in Sociology at Cambridge and, later, the first Chairman of the Social Science Research

Council. 'Been there, done that' would be a good definition of Michael Young or, since 1977, Lord Young of Dartington in recognition of all his contributions to society.

Why Dartington? Because Dartington School and its founders, the Elmhirsts, were to be key to his early development and Michael was later to be a trustee of Dartington Hall for fifty years. He went there, aged fourteen, after a miserable childhood: squabbling and, ultimately, separated parents, a dreadful first boarding-school where the headmaster beat the boys naked in public and where his mother never visited. Always hungry, unloved and, at one stage, offered for adoption, he was a poor small waif of a lad. Luckily there were his father's kin in Australia. His grandmother had him to stay when he was four and about to be abandoned, and later there was his aunt who was interested in progressive education. It was she who rescued him from that boarding-school and found one slightly better, then discovered Dartington and persuaded the Australian grandfather to pay for it. 'I often think that my interest in "kinship studies" was a way of repaying the debt I owed to some of my own extended family.'

Dartington was perfectly suited to the budding young entrepreneur. 'It was like a bursting blossom.' There were hardly any formal lessons, the food was wonderful, everyone was encouraged to do things themselves. For Michael that meant setting up a poultry company – Darfowls – and then a vegetable business, selling to the school, and another one repairing motor cycles. 'It was such great fun to be there.' He was lucky, too, as it turned out, that his parents didn't want to see him in the holidays, so Dorothy Elmhirst, the founder of the school with her husband, Leonard, brought him under her wing. American and hugely rich by inheritance, Dorothy Elmhirst took him to the United States every holiday, including a stay each time at the White House with her friend Eleanor Roosevelt. Dartington did not suit everyone but for Michael it was conclusive evidence that education can transform lives.

He left the school full of confidence and went to train as a lawyer. 'It will suit you because you're so argumentative,' one of his teachers told him. But it was not his cup of tea, as it turned out, although it proved useful later on. Instead, he enrolled for a degree in economics at the LSE and started working at PEP (Political and Economic Planning) where he became Director. From there he went to the Research Department of the Labour Party in time for the 1945 election. That experience introduced him to all the senior political figures of the left, but also convinced him that he was not going to be suited to the hustings and the political life. He could do more to change things, he reckoned, by working on the edge. Michael went off to found the Institute of Community Studies in Bethnal Green, living on £4 a week, with three colleagues. So started his life long journey of continuous alchemy.

So far there had been no major slips in his career. Not all ideas work out, however, and one of Michael's favourites, his plan to use the unused part of the university year at Cambridge to run an alternative university, taught by distance-learning methods, ran up against an entrenched Cambridge Establishment. Nothing daunted, Michael founded the National Extension College there, the forerunner of the Open University. And so it continued to the grand total of forty-nine new creations, not all of which succeeded, although a remarkable number are still going strong. Even now, in his eighties, Michael is sprouting ideas for new projects. 'I can't stop thinking of what appear to be worthwhile ideas. They seem so obvious.'

Michael remembers that it was all work in his thirties and forties, long hours and not much money or time to support his family. So it always is for those with a mission or a passion. As personalities, they are often difficult to live or work with, their ideas compelling but demanding, their energy exhausting to keep up with. Michael does not know the meaning of self-indulgence. A business lunch turns out to be a bowl of soup in a tiny kitchen in Victoria Park Square. Expert in raising money for his creations, he is uninterested in it for himself.

Michael is unique. He was lucky, he admits – in his Dartington education, in his patron, Dorothy Elmhirst, in the attention his early writings generated – but 'luck', he says, 'sort of happens if you know what you want'. He is the ultimate 'unreasonable man', never taking no for an answer, convinced, 'that anything is possible.' Yes, but you need Michael's power of persuasion and dogged determination to turn the possible into successful action.

Epilogue

This book is a work of celebration about the achievements of ordinary people who have gone on to do extraordinary things. The hope is that they will inspire others to do likewise and will encourage those who run our cities, our schools and our governments to reflect on how to nurture more people like them.

Reflecting on the interviews as a whole, however, some interesting issues emerge, ones to which the research provided no obvious answers. They are, nevertheless, important topics for policy makers, in both government and large organizations, to reflect upon as well as for the alchemists, and others like them, to consider, as they ponder their own futures.

There are, we realized, no manufacturing businesses in our list, for Trevor Baylis's inventions are made in South Africa and Joanne McFarlane's silk scarf venture has not yet extended beyond her bedroom. Was this our sampling error, or did it represent something more significant?

We focused only on alchemists in London. London is an expensive site for any manufacturing business, particularly one that aspires to grow. In that respect our research was perhaps unrepresentative of the country as a whole. Another possibility is that manufacturing can no longer rely on single individuals for innovation. Sir Alec Broers of Cambridge argues that, in these sophisticated days, while a scientific or technological idea may originate with one person it needs a network and an institution to bring it to fruition. Trevor Baylis in this study, or James Dyson with his vacuum cleaner are, therefore, smaller-scale exceptions. Our list, which is confined to individual alchemists, would not have picked up the larger team-based or institutional innovations. It would also explain why we had difficulty in finding any individual alchemists in the medical or pure science areas.

The reason for the scarcity of manufacturing alchemists may, however, be more to do with finance. Manufacturing and scientific

233

enterprises require larger amounts of initial money, partly because more people are likely to be involved. Knowledge or service businesses are low-entry-cost ventures. Because of Britain's relative lack of venture capital funds, or of banks willing to support expensive ideas unless they in turn are backed by substantial assets, it is the knowledge or service enterprises that are more likely to get started, businesses that only require outside funds when already well established. None of the ventures we examined needed initial outside funding.

It would, though, be disquieting if the lack of manufacturing examples turned out to be an indicator of a country-wide aversion to the alchemy of things as opposed to that of services of all sorts. Economies everywhere, it is true, are moving from manufacturing to services but it is harder to export the latter and to grow them internationally except by merging with competitors in other countries, the so-called strategic alliances, which now proliferate in financial and consulting firms. Service-based economies with no manufacturing component may, therefore, be condemning themselves to low-growth futures. Silicon Valley has proved that manufacturing alchemy can succeed, having seen the birth of firms such as Intel, 3Com, Netscape and many others, mostly started by one individual, which are all now global corporations. We have too few counterparts in Britain.

We have already noted that none of our alchemists aspired to be the equivalent of Rupert Murdoch, dominating the media world. But we wondered, on reflection, why this was and why it was that none of them saw himself or herself as starting a family firm in the tradition, for example, of Italy where family business dynasties last for centuries.

We came across no equivalent to Bill Gates, no one who thought that the business would one day be a huge global corporation. Tim Waterstone, it is true, hoped to see his name on a bookstore in every major city and Richard Branson's brand is now world-wide, but neither is thinking of great global public companies. There is, in fact, a general puzzlement about the failure of the British to build vast businesses from small beginnings, something that the Americans do so much better.

Is it because the alchemists lack the huge ambitions that would propel such growth? Or is it because it is so much harder to grow a service business internationally, as Anita Roddick, among many others, found out when she expanded into the American market. The fast-growth American firms are all manufacturers of some sort. Maybe manufacturing growth is easier to achieve, although McDonald's is living proof that it can be done from a service base. Or is it, perhaps, more comfortable to stick with what you know and can control? To grow exponentially and internationally inevitably results in a loss of direct control and the end of the family culture.

It was our impression that the alchemists we studied were more interested in doing what they believed in and enjoyed, than in bestriding the world in their field, starting a dynasty, or in amassing huge piles of money. Is this good or bad? Bad for the economy, perhaps, but not necessarily for society, which has the benefit of businesses run by people who care enough about what they do to let the company bear their name.

Perhaps, too, the lack of any need to create a family business that would span the generations, if not the centuries, is because they do not want to choose their children's destinies for them. From those alchemists with families we got the impression that the family and the business were separate entities, both important but not intertwined. It does, however, give rise to the next issue.

We met the alchemists at the height of their success. More is yet to come, no doubt. But one day they will leave, retire, or even die. What then happens to their organizations since they do not appear to be planning dynasties? Is alchemy a short-lived flower, or can its creations bloom for ever under someone else?

Most of those we met had a low tolerance of boredom. That seems to be true of most creative people, which is why doggedness is a necessary complement to their dedication and desire to make a difference if anything is to happen. But doggedness is tolerable only because of the dedication. What happens when that goes? Martin Leach, for one, is clear that he is happier when starting new ventures than he is running them, so he will always sell them on and begin something new. It wasn't always clear what would happen to the other organizations when dedication ran out and the alchemist moved on.

One feature of growing firms is that the founder often turns out not to be the best person to build the business once it has got going. The style of management that is needed has to change at that stage, to become more formal and more regulated, less an extension of the personality of the originator, more formally professional. The transition is difficult and is seldom achieved without pain. Yet if it isn't done the organization will wither and die when the founder leaves or loses interest. We wondered about the long-term future of some of the ventures we encountered, although there were no signs at present that any of the founders was bored.

All the alchemists played to their strengths. That was one secret of their success. But strengths tend to have their opposites. Passion and dedication, for example, are, as we saw, essential for successful alchemy, but they can also be blinkers, blinding one to the world beyond the immediate task. We wondered, therefore, whether our alchemists, either now or in the future, would be sufficiently open to the weaknesses of their strengths.

Terence Conran is a hugely successful designer, an individual creating both products and enterprises out of his very personal passion and imagination. He found, however, that he was not using enough of those strengths when he was running a big conglomerate. He now concentrates once more on design and the generation of projects which he lets others run. Richard Branson has proved to be acute in starting new businesses where he sees a need. Until recently, however, he had never tried to turn around a large existing company. With Virgin Rail he now has this challenge. He is confident that he will succeed but it may be that he will find that beginning something from scratch is very different from working from an inherited base.

Those who are adept at creating organizations in their own image, as is true of all those men and women whom we met, may be bad at running other people's with different values or perspectives. Which is why, perhaps, they instinctively keep their ventures small enough to be reflections of themselves and are noticeably reluctant to hand control to outsiders such as institutional shareholders. This will, however, ultimately hinder their growth, as we noticed above.

Those who are good at listening are often bad at deciding and vice versa. Some learn by studying documents, reports and numbers, some by talking with others. If your favourite way of learning does not fit the needs of the situation then your strength becomes a weakness. Too much time studying the figures can mean that one ignores the more informal signals that come from interacting with people and the reverse is also true – too much talk can mean the numbers get neglected. Or a passion for something – tailoring in the case of Ozwald Boateng, for example – may lead one to be inattentive to the finances of the business.

Can a powerful personality hear discordant voices? All our alchemists insisted that they were open to ideas and encouraged a wide debate among their staff. We have no reason to doubt their beliefs but, given their wish to recruit like-minded people to work with them, it must be a problem to find much disagreement. Yet discordant voices can be salutary, sometimes 'people like us' can be too consensual. Different and maverick the alchemists might be themselves, but we wondered how well they would tolerate, even encourage, mavericks of a different mind from theirs.

It is a difficult balance to achieve – building a community of like-minded people while still listening to those who disagree, to be dedicated to what one is doing, yet to have time to walk in other worlds and hear other voices in other places. This diversity in their lives is what John McLaren and Sabrina Guinness try to achieve and what others would like to find more often. Julian Richer devotes at least one third of his time to charitable causes. These activities probably refresh him as much as they benefit others. William Atkinson spends some of his time on national and international forums, away from his school. Again, in addition to the expertise he brings to these committees and gatherings, he himself must benefit from the broader perspective it gives him.

It is essential if the futures of their organizations are ever going to be different from their past, that their founders find the time to step outside the boxes they have created for themselves.

If alchemy is so necessary does it always have to start in fresh pastures? Can alchemists inhabit worlds that they do not themselves create? Can institutions, in other words, grow their own alchemists?

On the evidence of our sample the answer must be 'no', unless, like Dennis Stevenson, they enter at the top. Yet many organizations seek to cultivate their 'intrapreneurs' with rewards for innovative ideas, 'skunk works' for experiments and think tanks off site. The record on these is patchy. More commonly, organizations buy in their alchemy once it has been proved elsewhere, hoovering up small innovative companies that have been alchemical in their time but whose founders now want out and are prepared to sell their secrets to a bigger corporation that will know how to exploit them. The record shows that if the alchemist is asked to stay on to manage his or her old business it doesn't work. The alchemist becomes a thorn in the side of the acquiring organization and eventually leaves, depressed and angry.

This seems a waste of talent. It would be preferable to see large companies fund some external alchemy from the outset rather than buying up the successful when much of the doggedness and dedication may have evaporated. Businesses could be more like venture capitalists, fertilizing alchemy rather than merely hoping to harvest it. We wondered why it didn't happen more often.

In Summary

There is much that we don't know about alchemy, even after a concentrated year of talking to some outstanding practitioners. They themselves do not find it easy to explain – how do you make clear the way to ride a bicycle to someone who has never been on one? Those who know it can only demonstrate, not elucidate. Which is why there are some unanswered questions and why, in the end, we can only learn by watching others and then imitate, practise and make it our own. The best that we, the authors, can do is to make it fashionable to try, for fashion is still one of the most powerful agents of change in every field, including that of business and social organizations.

The Alchemy Award

The Alchemy award has been created by the charity, Common Purpose, whose founder Julia Middleton, is featured in this book.

The Award will be given to the person who, in the opinion of a panel of judges, has provided the best example of alchemy, be it in the area of business, the arts, the social community or any other sphere.

It is the hope of the sponsors that the Award will promote the spread of alchemy and alchemists in the UK.